Cantares: Canticles and Poems of Youth

1925-1932

Recovering the U.S. Hispanic Literary Heritage

Board of Editorial Advisors

Cantares: Canticles and Poems of Youth 1925-1932

Fray Angélico Chávez

Edited, with an introduction, by
Nasario García

With a Foreword by E. A. Mares

Recovering the U.S. Hispanic Literary Heritage

Arte Público Press
Houston, Texas

This volume is made possible through grants from the Rockefeller Foundation and the City of Houston through the Cultural Arts Council of Houston, Harris County.

Recovering the past, creating the future

Arte Público Press
University of Houston
Houston, Texas 77204-2174

Cover design by Adelaida Mendoza
Cover photo courtesy of Museum of New Mexico, Neg. No. 132819

Chávez, Fray Angélico, 1910–1996.
Cantares: Canticles and Poems of Youth—1925–1932 /
by Fray Angélico Chávez; edited by Nasario García.
p. cm. — (Recovering the U.S. Hispanic Heritage Series)
ISBN 1-55885-311-1 (pbk. : alk. paper)
1. Christian poetry, American. 2. Hispanic Americans—Poetry.
3. New Mexico—Poetry. I. García, Nasario. II. Title. III. Recovering the U.S. Hispanic Literary Heritage Project publication.
PS3505.H625 C54 2000
811'.52—dc21 00-056587
CIP

The paper used in this publication meets the requirements of the American National Standard for Information Sciences—Permanence of Paper for Printed Library Materials, ANSI Z39.48-1984.

Printed in the United States of America

0 1 2 3 4 5 6 7 8 9 10 9 8 7 6 5 4 3 2 1

Dedicated to
The family of Fray Angélico Chávez

Contents

Foreword xi

Acknowledgments xv

Introduction xvii

Cantares de Cíbola

Cantares 3
The Desert Artist 3
Pegasus 4
The Paintings 4
A Poet's House 5
Cinquains to the Padre 5
I Wondered and I Asked Myself 6
The Painting Poet 7
"Foreign" New Mexico 7
On the Alameda 9
Roses 9
Mountain Padres 9
Night in the Canyon 10
City of Saint Francis 10
A Burro on the Plaza 11
Santa Fe Skyline 11
The Deserted Mission 12
My Country 12
The Archbishop's Garden 13
Cross of the Friar-Martyrs 14
Dawn at the Missions 14
Dust 16
Navajo 16
The Mission Guadalupe 17
A Song of the Padre 18
The Worshippers 18
Fray Serra 20
A Litany of Pueblos 20
In the Arms of the Pine Tree 22
Ácoma 24
Pecos Ruins 24
A Dance in Cochití 25
Cíbola's Cathedral 25
Wings of Death 26

Saint Michael's Window 27
Go With God 27
Parable 28
Ballad of a Fiddler 28
Tango 29

Cantares de María

The Lady of the Snows 36
May Gems 37
Queen of the Friars Minor 37
Our Lady's First Communion 37
Sermons in Stones 38
Dolores 39
For a Valentine 40
An Idyll Belvedere 40
Thou Heardest First My Lullaby 42
A Carol Mystic 42
Madonna by Murillo 43
On a Street-car 44
The Priestess 44
The Visitation 45
Doncella 45
A La Conquistadora (Spanish) 47
The Virgin of Guadalupe 48
Esther 48
Hyacinth 50
Mother's Day 50
Christmas Lullaby 50
A Legend of the Holy Family— 51

Cantares Franciscanos

Brown Shadow 54
Stigmata of Saint Francis 54
Il Ricchio Poverello 55
The Friar's Christmas Gift 55
The Jester's Carol 57
Serus in Coelum Redeas 57
Franciscan Poet 58
Silly Lyric 58
In Memoriam 59
To Saint Paschal 60
A Seraphic Serenade 61
Little Poor Man To Little Boy Blue 66
The Fairy Friar 66
Joannis Duns Scoti (Latin) 68
Jesum Liliaque (Latin) 69
Ventramour 70
Legend of the Bl. Ramón Lull, O.F.M. 70
Sonnet to a Modern Young Lady 71
Father and Son Before Saint Anthony 71
Franciscans in China 72
If Miracles 73
Antonian Thoughts 73
Hymn of the Brown Marines 74

Vision of Fray del Alba— 75
Vignettes
Son of Bouillon 81
The Son of St. Augustine 82
The Son of St. Francis 83
The Son of the Testament 85
The Son of the Eucharist 86
The Son of Nature 87
The Barefoot Boy 88

Cantares Varios

Canticle of the Rainbow 90
Jesus at the Well 92
To Witter Bynner 92
A New Year Lyric 93
Christmas in Heaven 93
Little Christmas 94
Ruth 96
The Holy Innocents 96
Simon Peter 97
Saint Therese 97
First Poem 97
Mother 97
Seminarian's Prayer 98
The Little Flower 98
Prayers 99
Even Song 99
Chancel Light 100
At Night 100
I Sat with Sorrow 101
Books 102
Sonnet 102
My Shepherd-Host 103
The Voice of Dismas 103
Makers of the Cross 104
At Calvary 105
Easter Lilies 106
Priesthood 106
Departure 106
Golden Stairs 107
Reformation 107
Midsummer Night's Drean 108
Thanatopsis 108
Communion 108
Trees 109
A Shooting-Star 109
The Old Organ 110
The Loving Shepherd 110
Mighty Builders 111
Portrait of a Catechist 111
To a Young Seminarian 111
The Rondeau 112
Wake Me the Birds 113
Ring Easter Bells 113
The Hiders 114
Surprised 114
Lines 114
Reassured 115

'Twas the Last Rose . . . 115
Sonnet from the Spanish of Calderón 116
Prisoner 116
Beauty and the Hidden Truth 117
Oculos Habent 117
The Wren 118
To a Diminutive Chickadee 118
The Pagan 119
Giralda 120
The Angelus 121
At the Holy Sepulchre 121
VI Station 122
Catholic Negro Spiritual 122
Advertisement 123
Death of a Virgin 124
Baptism 125
Eucharistic Rubáiyát 125
What Little Flower 126
Shepherds 126
To a Little Orphan Girl 127
The Humblest Saint 128
Tabernacle Scene 128
Love's Tender Prisoner 129
Sonnet of the Via Crucis 129
Hymn to Saint Louis 130
Heritage 130
All for Love 131
Books by Fray Angélico Chávez 133

Foreword

The New York Times obituary of Fray Angélico Chávez, dated March 22, 1996, mentions his poetry and his painting, but it emphasizes his historical contributions rather than his literary merits. Angélico Chávez's historical work is, of course, very important, and it is fitting and appropriate that the Archdiocese of New Mexico dedicated its archives to this man who so painstakingly cataloged them. His paintings were also remarkable. Nevertheless, an equally strong case could be made for considering Angélico Chávez a significant literary figure, particularly as a poet, not only for New Mexico but also for the world.

Now, with the publication of *Cantares*, a first book of poems, many never before circulated to the general public, we are privileged to read the earliest poetry of Angélico Chávez, which confirms his extraordinary talent as a poet.

The title *Cantares* means "songs" or "chants" in the most elementary sense, harkening back to the biblical "Cantar de los Cantares," or the Song of Songs, and to the medieval ballads of great deeds or exploits, the "cantares de gesta." Although the book's original table of contents does not mention it, this collection is actually divided into four parts: "Cantares de Cíbola," "Cantares de María," "Cantares Franciscanos," and "Cantares Varios."

In 1932, Duns Scotus College bound a typewritten copy of these poems of Angélico Chávez, or Manuel Ezequiel Chávez (his given name before he adopted the name of Fra Angélico de Fiesole, the famed 15th-century Italian artist and priest). Only twenty-two at the time, Chávez still had several years of study ahead before he would become a Franciscan, but he was already a gifted and accomplished poet. In fact, Chávez wrote all the *Cantares* poems from age fifteen to twenty-two. Clearly, few poets so young could produce such a readable, sophisticated book of poems—a feat especially impressive in that this work is still worth reading almost three-quarters of a century after the poems were written.

From the very first poem in *Cantares* to the last, certain salient characteristics of Fray Angélico's youthful work can be seen. A well-developed craftsmanship, deep religious beliefs, and consummate lyrical sense all contribute to his unique style.

It would be hard to find a cumbersome line in Fray Angélico's poems. He uses vivid images and comparisons, and has a sharp eye for detail. With rhyme, slant rhyme, and internal rhyme, he writes ballads, sonnets, and cinquains.

The cinquain, invented by the American poet Adelaide Crapsey, is an unrhymed form worth mentioning because it illustrates the technical grasp of the young poet. Plus, Chávez exhibits a wide range, from classical Greek and Latin, to the Spanish mystics, especially Santa Teresa de Jesús, to the contemporary period. His poems show a keen awareness of major Western painters, particularly Spanish and French. At an early age, Angélico Chávez was already a master of form and structure who was at ease with all major elements of craftsmanship.

Of course, the young Angélico Chávez was not a flawless poet. He occasionally falls into easy rhymes and an irritating singsong iambic syllabic stress pattern, and is at times very sentimental in his verse. His poems about the Pueblos and other indigenous people reveal that he shared the views of a dying Spanish colonial interpretation of the past. The Pueblos are mere pretexts for poems praising the saints whose names were imposed by the Spaniards on those they had conquered. When these poems were written, Angélico Chávez's world view was hierarchical, and Christianity was viewed as a gift delivered to people at a low level of cultural and religious development. This stand was common among educated *nuevomejicanos* in the 1930s and 1940s.

Nevertheless, it would be historically provincial to dismiss his quality poems simply because they reflected his own social and historic milieu. Furthermore, his biography of Padre Antonio José

Martínez of Taos, *But Time and Chance,* was notewrothy in rebuilding and reinterpreting a period of New Mexico's intellectual history that might otherwise have been lost.

From his earliest poems it is obvious that some deep sense of spirituality animated Angélico Chávez's work. What matters here is not that he was religious. After all, there are millions of the faithful with certifiably tin ears. Rather, what is important is that Angélico Chávez was able to express his religious fervor in truly dynamic imagery, as in the poem "A Shooting Star" where a shooting star is compared to Lucifer "proud falcon of the sky" who is slain by the Hunter (God) and falls from his "boastful flight," tumbling headlong "followed by/ a spray of feathers flashing/ in the night!" In poem after poem with religious content, Angélico Chávez works and re-works the traditional imagery, biblical imagery, for example, and refracts it, bends it, through the prism of his own poetic vision, and returns it to the world in his own voice, his own poem. Above all, Angélico Chávez was a lyrical poet. While many of the poems in *Cantares* have a narrative base, what is truly impressive in them is the powerful lyricism that runs like a rushing mountain current from poem to poem. In "The Wren," for example, God, after creating the world, rests and "wishing to play, he fluted out a hollow reed." Soon, "a crumpled feather from some nest" wanders into the reed, and "God smiled and blew; there came a/ squeak/ With quirking tail and wings and breast." "In The Arms of the Pine Tree" looks down from the arms of a pine tree on a mountain to a valley below where two willows grow by a fountain. The scene reminds the poet of his childhood, and he says of the willows:

> In the cool of the fountain, in whose
> depths the willows tresses
> Dip their olive-green reflections, I
> once knew the nestling's bliss;
> In their intertwining branches, down
> their emerald caresses,
> I had stooped to childhood's fountain
> and received a crystal kiss.

Such lyricism is prevalent throughout *Cantares.* These are poems to be read for the sheer pleasure of reading them. Most of them are as fresh today as the day they were written long ago. That is what good poetry is all about.

E. A. Mares
Albuquerque, NM

Acknowledgments

Each book that one publishes has its proper genesis, its own evolution and reason for coming to fruition. Ideas for any published work quite often spring forth in the most unpredictable of ways—some even lodged in unsuspected portions of the human spirit. The time of day or night when these ideas are born at times can perhaps surprise if not amaze the scholar or creative writer.

In Fray Angélico Chávez collection of poetry, *Cantares: Canticles and Poems of Youth 1925–1932,* his creative precocity comes to light at a very tender age. His poetic genius manifests itself in subsequent poetry that he published throughout his lifetime in periodicals and books. *Cantares,* on the other hand, because of the author s wishes, was held in abeyance and not for public dissemination until after his death.

Therefore, I was deeply honored when Tom E. Chávez, Fray Angélico's nephew and Director, Palace of the Governors in Santa Fe, and caretaker of *Cantares,* asked if I would be interested in publishing his uncle's collection of poetry. His magnanimous gesture in providing me the opportunity to edit and to publish Fray Angélico's only known unpublished creative work is, to say the least, extremely gratifying. *Cantares* has enabled me in a very special way to play a small yet fortuitous part in the Fray Angélico's scholarly, artistic, and creative universe.

My fond memories of the correspondence Fray Angélico and I had three years prior to his death regarding his life cannot go unrecognized. Even in failing health, he took precious time from his daily routine to write to me. An exchange of letters between his brother Antonio "Tony" E. Chávez and me regarding Fray Angélico's personality and intellect as I prepared *Cantares* for publication is hereby acknowledged as well.

A special note of appreciation goes to Richard V. Teschner, who suggested Professor Emeritus John M. Sharp's name to me, and to John M. Sharp himself—both from the University of Texas at El Paso—for his gracious help in translating two of the poems from Latin to English.

My heartfelt thanks also go to Nicolás Kanellos, Publisher, Arte Público Press, for his kind willingness to publish a worthy and meritorious collection of poetry from one of the Land of Enchantment's premier poets and foremost Hispanists.

Finally, and of no lesser consequence, I wish to express my sincere appreciation to Gabriela Baeza Ventura, Executive Editor, Arte Público Press, for lending a helping hand every step of the way, and to her staff for their generous and gracious assistance in seeing *Cantares* become a reality in order for Fray Angélico Chávez aficionados and the general public to enjoy.

Introduction

Fray Angélico Chávez: A Man of Many Talents

This introduction is divided into three parts. The first segment acquaints the reader with Fray Angélico Chávez by providing a sequence of events in his life beginning in Wagon Mound, New Mexico, where he was born, until he passed away in Santa Fe. In reviewing special moments in his illustrious career as priest, scholar, artist, creative writer, and archivist, we see the portrait of a multitalented person emerge in full bloom. The second portion offers an overview of Fray Angélico's world of literary prose and the genius behind his poetry. The final section, which is of fundamental importance, is the presentation of his *Cantares: Canticles and Poems of Youth—1925–32*, his first book-length collection of poems, which he wrote as a young boy, from age fifteen to twenty-two.

I never met Fray Angélico Chávez personally, but in 1993, although terminally ill, he was still energetic and spunky enough to chat over the phone and correspond with me by mail. My intentions at that time were to tape-record him for a book on Hispano writers of New Mexico, but his energy level had reached a low ebb, and he thus declined to sit down for a live interview. He refused because, as he wrote me, "Now I find [even] all reading most difficult, due to a tumor that has been discovered at the top of my brain! So I find the book you sent me [*Recuerdos de los viejitos: Tales of the Río Puerco*] most difficult to read. In fact, I cannot read newspapers except for the headlines."[1] Instead of handwritten responses to my questions, he opted to send me his own *recuerdos*. He said, "I had started this 'family' history since you first contacted me. After receiving your beautiful *Recuerdos*, I finished these *recuerdos* of mine with these last couple of pages."

Consequently, I abandoned my quest to include him in my book *Pláticas: Conversations with Hispano Writers of New Mexico,* published recently by Texas Tech University Press. Even he recognized that for a man in his 80s, both the physical stamina and intellectual acumen—the trademarks of a stellar career as churchman, scholar, and humanist—were no longer inner parts of his persona.

As if to soothe the aborted exchange of words between us, he sent me a copy of his book *Chávez: A Distinctive American Clan of New Mexico,* with the following inscription: "Para el buen autor Nasario García. Con admiración de la raza" [For the good author Nasario García. With the admiration of our people]. Hence, our brief but enjoyable correspondence came to an abrupt end.

Fray Angélico Chávez [Manuel Ezequiel Chávez], the eldest of ten children, was born in Wagon Mound, New Mexico, on April 10, 1910, to Fabián Chávez, Sr., and Nicolasa Roybal de Chávez. After a brief illness, he died in Santa Fe on March 18, 1996—a month short of his eighty-sixth birthday—thus bringing to a close a long and celebrated career. New Mexico lost not only a native son, but also one of its most shining treasures, and his recognition and popularity, sometimes colored by controversy due to his forthright nature, transcended the boundaries. Upon Chávez's passing, Robert McG. Thomas, Jr. of the *New York Times* wrote, "Fray Angélico Chávez [was] a multitalented Franciscan priest whose outpouring of poems, paintings, stories and historical writings celebrated and chronicled the early history of New Mexico . . ." (of March 1966).

From the onset Fray Angélico's parents encouraged their children to seek an education. His father attended a Wagon Mound private school, run by Don Zeferino Trujillo, who was educated in France and subsequently brought back by Bishop Jean Baptiste Lamy. His mother, Nicolasa Roybal, attended what is today known as New Mexico Highlands University in Las Vegas; she then returned to Wagon Mound, where she taught elementary school prior to marrying Fabián Chávez, Sr., in 1909. Fray Angélico's own words show how his parents emphasized education from the time he was a small boy. "My parents," he wrote me, "were avid readers, and had certain books, both of which habits influenced me in reading. There was an illustrated Spanish booklet for children by which I began learning the language correctly. I also remember reading a book of poems by Julio Arboleda, a famous Mexican poet of those times. Besides English primary textbooks, there was a set of the *Columbia Encyclopedia* into which I dug even if beyond my ken in childhood days. All this got me into a reading habit by the time I was five. I had learned good English as well as Spanish before I went to public school" (Fray Angélico).

Throughout his writing career, virtually everything that he wrote and published was in English, but his competence in Spanish, his mother tongue, as attested to by his archival research of Spanish documents, was undeniable. Along the way, he also learned Greek, German, and Latin, but, according to his brother Antonio (Tony) Chávez, Fray Angélico was quite adept at discussing psychology, philosophy, poetry, and the mystics. His familiarity with the classics was also quite phenomenal.[2] Despite his multi-linguistic abilities and obvious fondness for languages, Fray Angélico viewed English as the most beautiful language in the world.[3]

As a child he showed certain precocious tendencies, as well as a curiosity for inquiry, that led, in great measure, to his being inspired to become a Franciscan priest while recognizing that he was blessed with creative, artistic, and scholarly talents. He was but a tot when he found himself in southern California in a "foreign" land away from his native New Mexico. "[My] parents took me to San Diego, California [1911–1916], where Father did carpentry [Fabián Chávez, Sr., learned carpentry from his own father, Eugenio Chávez] for the Panama-Pacific Exposition, especially the Grant Hotel. I learned *only English* by the time we returned to Wagon Mound at the end of 1916. There in San Diego I first heard of Fray Junípero Serra, and the *Franciscan idea* first got hold in my mind, if only vaguely" (Fray Angélico).

Subsequently, a set of mitigating circumstances came into play—a kind of a catharsis ensued—that shaped his future career as a Franciscan priest. In 1917 Fray Angélico found himself back in Mora, New Mexico, one of the most idyllic and beautiful regions in the state, where his father was twice elected county clerk as a Democrat in a strong Republican county. Fray Angélico's "penchant for reading and writing" increased, as well as his respect for the Loretto Sisters in the Mora public schools. He not only looked upon them as "great teachers of the old perfect methods," but it was they who inspired him in his reading and writing habits. "My reading," he boasted proudly, "taught me that the Franciscans had been the only clergy in New Mexico for two centuries, 1598–1798. This woke up my California dream of Fray Junípero Serra, and I dreamt of becoming a Franciscan myself!" (Fray Angélico).

But Fray Angélico's religious or spiritual calling transcended the Franciscan order. As mentioned above, he was well acquainted with the Spanish mystics, namely, the Carmelites San Juan de la Cruz and Santa Teresa de Jesús (1515–1582) from Avila, whom he revered. In her spiritual biography, *El libro de su vida,* published posthumously in 1588, which she preferred to call *El libro de las misericordias de Dios,* she not only shares with the world at large a litany of spiritual experiences, but also declares her resolute devotion to God in this way:

> Since this new death-in-life I've known,
> Estrang'd from self my life has been,
> For now I live a life unseen:
> The Lord has claim'd me as His own.
> My heart I gave Him for His throne,
> Whereon He wrote indelibly:
> *'I die because I do not die."*[4]

Like Santa Teresa de Jesús (Teresa de Cepeda y Blásquez de Ahumada) 400 years before him, Fray Angélico Chávez in 1929 declared himself a servant of God, and from the principles inherent in the Franciscan Order, he never deviated. Testimony to his religious vows and commitment to God can be gleaned from the poem "I Vowed," published in 1939, two years after his ordination:

I vowed that I would not possess
Things having bulk of earthly dross,
Because my Lord in emptiness
Lay in the crib and on the cross.[5]

Nevertheless, at age fourteen he had long before—in 1924, in fact—undertaken his seminary studies starting in September at Saint Francis Seraphic Seminary in Cincinnati, Ohio. Fray Angélico described 1924 as "a great year." His exuberance stemmed no doubt from the fact that he excelled in his studies. He did well for a "Mexican" among Germanics, as he put it, but once again acknowledged his indebtedness to both his parents and the Loretto Sisters for his academic success.

Following his stint as a high school seminarian, he became a novitiate of Saint John the Baptist Province of the Order of Friars Minor, also situated in the same city. But his studies in theology, including philosophy, one of his favorite subjects, took him to Detroit, Michigan, and Oldenburg, Indiana. Thereafter, he returned to his beloved state, where he was ordained a Franciscan priest on May 6, 1937, at Saint Francis Cathedral in Santa Fe, the same place where a memorial Mass was celebrated in his honor following his death. Fray Angélico had the rare if not enviable distinction of being the first native son ever to be ordained a Franciscan priest in the Land of Enchantment.

After his ordination, his first assignment was to Nuestra Señora de Guadalupe Parish in Peña Blanca along the Río Grande Valley southwest of Santa Fe, the state capital. His principal duty as missionary was to attend the three Keres Pueblos—namely, Cochití, Santo Domingo, and San Felipe—where he enjoyed carrying on the tradition of the Spanish Franciscans. In the process, not only did the Pueblo people like him, but his own love for them was also irrevocable. They particularly enjoyed the Indian expressions with which he peppered his sermons when celebrating Mass in the respective missions.

Fray Angélico also had an artistic flair. While a small boy growing up in Mora, New Mexico, between January 1917 and June 1924, he delved into pencil and pen drawing, but he also painted scenes with water colors. Later, as a seminarian in Cincinnati, he was given oil paints by a fellow student with no artistic talent. It was during that time that Fray Angélico painted a group of angels and saints for some new altars commemorating Corpus Christi. The rector was so impressed with the paintings that he dubbed him "Fra Angélico," after the famous Florentine artist Giovanni da Fiesole (1387–1455). In 1929, when Fray Angélico joined the Franciscan Order, which is also when seminarians received their Franciscan names, the rector named him Fra Angélico. Later he opted for the Spanish version, Fray Angélico Chávez, a pen name that remained with him the rest of his life.

His artistic talents served him well throughout his writing career. Not only did he do many of his own book illustrations, but in 1939, while serving as assistant pastor in Peña Blanca, he also painted life-size murals of the *Via Crucis* in the Peña Blanca Church, which he had thought "gloomy." With the exception of Christ, he used local people as models, including his own sisters. The paintings attracted the attention of famous artists from Santa Fe, many of whom often took friends to view them. Fray Angélico considered the frescoes his greatest artistic achievement. However, in 1987 the local padres thought differently and proceeded to raze the Peña Blanca Church, destroying the murals and claiming that they possessed no artistic value (perhaps the priests' self-avowed expertise forgot the man behind the paintings and his artistic deftness). Fray Angélico remained quiet and launched no formal protest, but privately there is no doubt that he seethed with bitter disappointment at the destruction of his murals. As his nephew Tom E. Chávez said to me, "He was deeply hurt. Those who were around him, and knew him well enough, will tell you that from the day of the destruction of those paintings, he changed, personality-wise, and everything else. That was a deep hurt that he took to death with him. I don't know how else to explain it. He never expressed that to me per se, but, then, I was the next generation still" (Tom E. Chávez).

His "tour of duty" in Peña Blanca lasted approximately six years—until 1943—when he was called to active duty in the U.S. Army while World War II was already well under way. His military service as a chaplain took him to Camp Chaffee, Arkansas (1943–1944), before he was transferred to Camp Stockton, California and on to Honolulu at the end of 1944. Thereafter, he was summoned to join the famous New York 77th (Statue of Liberty) Infantry Division and headed for the South Pacific, where he and fellow countrymen met head on the ravages of war as they made a number of beachhead landings on Guam and Leyte. His poetic yet poignant words in the ensuing verses accentuate the dehumanizing and impressionable effects heaped upon the human psyche stemming from wars involving nations and leaders gone mad if not berserk:

The giant-blooming cereus are out tonight
In rows of cross-shaped stars along an avenue
Of sentry palms beneath a phosphorescent sky,
A lovely sight to view, but, oh! the roots, the roots.

We saw them planted day by day not far apart,
Dank roots of mandrake foully mocking human forms,
Their twisted limbs and bloated bellies mottled dark
With mud and mildew, and their clotted sap like gore.

Forgive us, fellows, for forgetting what we know,
For letting earth's erasure banish what we saw.
But you we will remember blooming white, O souls
More glorious than the Pleiades or Southern Cross![6]

After World War II ended, seemingly couched in time and history, Fray Angélico remained in the U.S. Army Reserves from 1948–1952, until he was asked to join the New Mexico National Guard. Once again he was called upon to serve his country after the outbreak of the Korean conflict, but instead of going to the Orient, he was shipped to Europe. Here, he attained the rank of major in the army. From his military base in Germany, he ventured to Spain, where he visited the birthplaces of his ancestors. Among those visited were Toledo and small towns in La Mancha and Extremadura (he visited Valverde de la Llerena, birthplace of his first direct ancestor to come to New Mexico[7]), in addition to places near Santiago de Compostela and Burgos. In retrospect, his trip to the Iberan Peninsula was of paramount significance, for it would later play a major role in his historical research linking Spain to New Mexico. As testimonials to this *madre patria-patria chica* connection, one can list his classic opus *My Penitente Land: Reflections on Spanish New Mexico,* along with his highly acclaimed *Origins of New Mexico Families.*

Following the Korean War and his European tour of duty, Fray Angélico returned to New Mexico once more. This time the archdiocese assigned him to Jémez Pueblo, nestled in the foothills of the beautiful Jémez Mountains northwest of Albuquerque, where he remained for seven years—from 1952–1959—before accepting the pastorship of Saint Joseph's Parish in Cerrillos southwest of Santa Fe. He remained here until 1964, when he began to devote fulltime to his research activities, an endeavor he had delved into while at Jémez Pueblo.

In 1971, Fray Angélico relinquished his duties as a Franciscan priest, but continued his avowed loyalty to his religious order of years gone by. However, it was during his self-imposed "retirement," at age sixty-one, that he was called upon by the Archbishop of Santa Fe to undertake the seemingly insurmountable task of cataloguing the archives of the archdiocese. This responsibility lasted from 1971–1976. Having honored and fulfilled the archbishop's request, Fray Angélico once again gravitated back to his Franciscan roots and his brothers. He spent the last seven years of his life (1989–1996) at the Saint Francis Friary in Santa Fe.

During those years, in ritual-like fashion, he took daily strolls in downtown Santa Fe. Recognizable because of his black beret, Fray Angélico could be spotted easily as he headed for his morning coffee at the Plaza Café. Quite often he was seen having lunch at the San Francisco Street Bar and Grill, where he chatted with locals and total strangers while he sipped on his favorite scotch, "Chávez Roybal"

According to his nephew Tom E. Chávez, he relished these encounters and could be quite affable, hardly a stuffed shirt.

His uncle's own wry sense of humor surfaced from time to time in the most unpredictable ways. Perhaps in part from watching Jack Benny and George Burns, two of his favorite comics, he had a great sense of humor and enjoyed all kinds of jokes, according to his brother Antonio (Tony) Chávez. For example, his mother once remarked that a certain man of ill repute "was not so bad because he was good to this mother." Fray Angélico's reply was, "So was the Devil!" (Antonio Chávez). Even toward the end of his life, despite his illness, Fray Angélico did not lose his humorous touch.

Tom E. Chávez, over the course of time, has shared a number of anecdotes with me about his uncle's seemingly unpredictable nature. He likes to tell the story about walking into a Santa Fe restaurant where Fray Angélico, who was having lunch with a young woman, summoned him over and said: "Here! I want you to meet your new aunt."

Tom E. Chávez believed that his uncle often said things to "shock" people into realizing that he was human and down-to-earth, not just a humble Franciscan priest. For example, when Tom E. Chávez, director of the Palace of the Governors in Santa Fe, proposed the idea of naming the archives and photography library in his honor, his uncle objected strenuously. His stance was firm and unequivocal; naming anything in his honor while he was still alive was an illusive, if not fallacious, proposition. His brother Fabián Chávez then suggested that he would entertain the notion after he died. Fray Angélico's reaction was quick and swift. "After I'm dead, who gives a shit!"

Ironically, today the refurbished library bears his name—The Fray Angélico Chávez History Library and Photographic Archives—thanks to the efforts of Friends of the Palace and to his nephew's wishes to honor not just an uncle or a native son, but someone who had distinguished himself in humane letters and as a soldier of God. Almost as if to taunt his uncle after he passed away, although motivated more from love and admiration, Tom E. Chávez, friends, and family members also obtained funds for a life-size bronze statue of Fray Angélico, molded and installed in front of the library for passersby to view and admire.

Never one to seek notoriety or to cast the spotlight on himself, Fray Angélico garnered, nevertheless, numerous awards, including honorary doctorates from both of the state's flagship institutions—The University of New Mexico and New Mexico State University. These were conferred for his lifelong accomplishments and contributions as a scholar and creative writer. In 1992, four years before his death, Spain's Juan Carlos de Borbón bestowed upon him the prestigious medal of the Order of Isabel la Católica for long-standing contributions to Hispanic culture in his native state of New Mexico. No gesture or recognition could have been more propitious or timely, given Fray Angélico's love for Spain and her connection to his own native Land of Enchantment. Since his death, the Center for Regional Studies at the University of New Mexico, in collaboration with the General Library, and under the auspices of the Center for Southwest Research, has established the Fray Angélico Chávez Fellowship, in recognition of his remarkable work as an historian.

When Chávez died, his Franciscan brethren took full charge of funeral arrangements, an overt yet silent manifestation of the respect and admiration they had for one of their own. But silence was not to be the order of the day, as accolades poured from all corners of New Mexico and beyond its borders. From public figures including President Bill Clinton, scholars, creative writers, to family members, to the media and members of the Catholic Church, the words of praise all had the same ring of adulation and respect for a consummate humanist. Few New Mexicans had ever equaled, let alone surpassed, his contributions as a scholar, creative artist, or churchman. Perhaps no one captured the essence and magnitude of his stature better than Santa Fe's Archbishop Michael Sheehan, who presided over the funeral Mass and proclaimed Fray Angélico's ubiquitous presence—from New Mexico to Spain, on to Mexico and other parts of Latin America. Fray Angélico Chávez was laid to rest at the friars' plot at Rosario Cemetery in Santa Fe on March 22, 1996.

Fray Angélico's Literary Prose and World of Poetics

While his voice was silenced on that fateful March 18, 1996, the trail of written words, both scholarly and creative, left behind as his legacy, will continue to shine upon us for a long time to come. To those familiar with his work, he is perhaps better known for his historical treatises and seminal articles on colonial New Mexican history. Notwithstanding his reputation as an historian, students of literature cannot afford to gloss over his creative world, both prose and poetry.

Among his first prose writings one can find *New Mexico Triptych—Being Three Panels and Three Accounts: 1. The Angel's New Wings; 2. The Penitente Thief; 3. Hunchback Madonna* (1940), three imaginary stories cast upon a medieval backdrop in northern New Mexico. *From an Altar Screen—El Retablo: Tales from New Mexico,* was published in 1957. These stories, humorous in tone, depicting the kinship between Hispanos of northern *New Mexico* and their patron saint, are reminiscent of Spain's medieval type *exempla. The Lady from Toledo,* Fray Angélico's only novel, was published for the first time in 1960. It is an historical account in which he weaves the story of Nuestra Señora de la Macana (originally called Nuestra Señora del Sagrario de Toledo), the events leading up to the Pueblo Revolt of 1680, and how she was rescued and returned for safe keeping to Mexico, where she still remains today.

Aside from his literary prose, it is poetry that Fray Angélico explored—and exploited—early on. At the Franciscan Seminary (1924–1929) in Cincinnati, Ohio, he became hooked on poetry when English professors introduced him to the writing of notable metaphysical writers Lord Byron and John Donne. His acquaintance with these poets, among others, enticed him to compose his own poems in "simple and pure language." Even after he joined the Franciscan Order in 1929, followed by his philosophical and theological studies from 1929–1937, his "side love of poetry" continued unabated.

In 1939, Fray Angélico's first book of poems, *Clothed With the Sun,* was published, although all but two of these poems had already appeared in a number of publications. The poetry is divided into three parts: Morning, Noon, and Night. *Clothed With the Sun*—also the title of one of his poems—was spearheaded by Witter Bynner, John Gould Fletcher,[8] Haniel Long, and Alice Corbin, the latter a co-founder of Poetry magazine. All of them were based in Santa Fe at the time, but were also nationally recognized literati whose poetry Fray Angélico had read and admired.

During World War II (1940–1943) he began publishing his poetry in New York literary magazines. Included among these were *America, Commonweal,* and *Spirit.* Three of his poems, "Southwestern Night," "Shepherds," and "Vineyard Song," which first appeared in *Spirit,* were later (1938, 1940, 1941) published in London in Thomas Moults' edition of *Best Poems of the Year.* Another poem, "Esther," was selected in 1946 by the famous London poet Alfred Noyes, for inclusion in his *Golden Book of Catholic Poetry.*

His second book of poetry, *Eleven Lady-Lyrics and Other Poems,* saw the light of day in 1946. Many of the poems in this collection were written prior to World War II and also printed previously in periodicals like *Commonweal* and *America;* others, such as those under the heading "With Poems of a War," were penned while he was serving in the military in the South Pacific and appeared in *Eleven Lady-Lyrics and Other Poems* for the first time.

Two years later, in 1948, he published *The Single Rose: the Rose Unica and Commentary of Fray Manuel de Santa Clara,* Santa Clara being the old name of his birthplace, Wagon Mound, New Mexico. It is clear that he used the rose, the most perfect of flowers, as a metaphor to convey the notion that achieving perfect spiritual harmony between man and God is indeed feasible.

The Virgin of Port Lligat (1959) is a long poem inspired by Salvador Dalí's painting in which Dalí expresses his own preoccupation with atomic warfare and its potential destruction to mankind. Ten years later, in 1969, Fray Angélico published his last book of poetry called *Selected Poems with An Apologia.* Like *Clothed with the Sun* thirty years earlier, many of the poems in *Apologia* had already been printed in various books and periodicals. The poems reflect in great measure his own introspective look at, and examination of, his own poetry—past and present. A kind of an apocalypse, a catharsis of sorts, came into play and prompted him later on—toward the end of World War II—to switch from prose and poetry to historical research. Thus, the poetic light that had long triggered his inspiration to create verses flickered and burned itself out.

Cantares: Canticles and Poems of Youth 1925–1932 The Beginning is the End

Cantares: Canticles and Poems of Youth—1925–1932, is a collection of poetry that Fray Angélico bequeathed to his parents in 1933 with the following inscription:

> A ustedes, mis queridos Padres,
> doy y dedico esta única colección
> de mis versos, no para que se la
> enseñen a todo el mundo, pero
> para que la guarden como señal
> de mi amor y devoción.
>
> Manuel
> 16 de agosto de 1933
> (Día de mi Profesión Solemne)

After his parents passed away, the collection changed hands among members of his family and was donated by his youngest brother and wife, José and Bernice Chávez, to the Fray Angélico History Library and Photographic Archives. Tom Chávez, as director of the Palace of the Governors in Santa Fe, and custodian of the library, made it available for publication. *Cantares*, assembled in 1932 while at Duns Scotus College, is Fray Angélico's first genuine body of poetry—and his last to be published, hence, "the beginning is the end." It is divided into: "Cantares de Cíbola," "Cantares de María,"

"Cantares Franciscanos," and "Cantares Varios." The total collection has one hundred sixty-eight poems. Of these, as far as can be ascertained, at least seventy have appeared in publications such as *America*, *Brown and White* (a publication of Saint Francis Seminary in Cincinnati), *Commonweal*, the *New Mexico Magazine*, *The New Mexico Sentinel*, and *The New York Times*. The preponderance of poems, based on an examination of Phyllis S. Morales' listings in *Fray Angélico Chávez: A Bibliography of His Published Writings (1925–1978)*, was printed in the *St. Anthony Messenger* between 1929 and 1965. However, approximately one hundred poems found in *Cantares* hitherto have remained unpublished and therefore are offered here for the first time.

The word *cantar* means "to sing." As a noun, it also denotes a couplet or brief poetic composition often accompanied by music. In looking across Spanish literature, the term cantar can be traced back to the Middle Ages with Spain's epic poem, *Cantar de Mío Cid* (1140), along with the word *juglar*. A *juglar* was the consummate public entertainer of the times (e.g., acrobat, musician, magician), who was perhaps best known as a reciter of poems, especially epic poems (*cantares de gesta*), in street corners, plazas, castles, and abbeys. He was, ostensibly, a professional actor who eked out an existence performing before public audiences.

Moreover, *cántico* (canticle), a derivative of cantar, and a poetic composition in which God is praised or given thanks (e.g., *Los cánticos de Moisés*), as well as *cantos*, in one fashion or another, have also figured prominently in literary titles among Spanish writers. The most notable are mystics such as Raimundo Lulio (1235–1315), best known for his mystical poem "Cántico del amigo y del amado," and San Juan de la Cruz, also a mystic whose "Cántico espiritual" is a running commentary on the meaning and significance of his poetry. Jorge Guillén, a well-known twentieth-century Spanish poet, also employed the term *cántico* in various editions of his *Cántico*. Furthermore, San Juan de la Cruz used the word *canciones* in "Canciones entre el alma y el esposo," in which he shows the relationship between the soul and God; plus, he also read Saint Gregory's "Song of Songs" ("Cantar de los Cantares"), a title that comes from the Bible.

Fray Angélico was no novice to Spanish literature. He was particularly well acquainted with Spain's Golden Age writers and fond of mystics such as Santa Teresa de Jesús and San Juan de la Cruz. It is little wonder, then, that he chose the word "cantares" and canticles as part of the main heading for his collection of poetry, *Cantares: Canticles and Poems of Youth—1925–1932*. Quite appropriate is that the first poem is titled "Cantares." There he sets forth the tone for the remaining poems contained in the first segment called "Cantares de Cíbola." "Cantares," like a magic wand, sparkle with metaphors and poetic imagery. In addition, Fray Angélico offers a kind of an apology for his modest poetic talent, and this is reminiscent of preambles written by Golden Age authors, including Miguel de Cervantes in *Don Quixote*. Fray Angélico writes:

> I weave a lariat of words
> To catch the Winged Horse;
> And with the cry of many birds
> It whistles in its course.
> But when my song is o'er, I fear
> I caught no horse with wings:
> For there's no Muse's lyre here
> It is the rope that sings.[9]

There is no particular reason why Fray Angélico labeled his first portion of poetry "Cantares de Cíbola," except to underscore, conceivably, an underlying historical footnote—that of the mythical Seven Cities of Cíbola which prompted in great measure the Spanish conquistadors' discovery of what is today New Mexico. The ventures of Francisco Vásquez de Coronado's journey and others who followed him in search of the mythical Seven Cities of Cíbola paved with gold and the treasures of the Gran Quivira helped establish the umbilical cord that ultimately stretched across the ocean waters connecting Spain and the Land of Enchantment. This partnership is made manifest in Fray Angélico's first repertoire of poems. Perhaps the poem that best captures this unbreakable bond between Spain and New Mexico is "My Country." In fact, one is left with the distinct if not unmistakable impression that the genesis for Fray Angélico's *My Penitente Land* is lodged in this poem. The poetics speak for themselves:

> Long ago saw the rovers Hellenic
> A land by the sunset bar,
>
> ....
>
> And the world recognized through the ages
> The beauty and might of Spain.
>
> Then the Padres joined hands with the angels
> And far to the sunset glow
> Carried part of the lovely 'España'
> And called her 'New Mexico." (*Cantares*)

But the poem "Tango," the last and longest in "Cantares de Cíbola," with the "singing of the charming tango," and "stepping to the wild fandango" as the "castanetting conifers re-echo thru the canyon," is another clear manifestation of the kinship between Spain and New Mexico that has endured into the twenty-first century. Still, Fray Angélico, even more than seventy years ago, bemoaned the lack of proper recognition of New Mexico and its beauty with an ironic twist seen in "'Foreign' New Mexico,"' "the eldest, yet the most young!" Curiously, this "foreignness," coupled with geographic ignorance by many people across this land, still plagues us to this day—eighty-eight years after New Mexico was admitted to the Union.

Another observation that can be made on a cursory level, without analyzing each poem, but endeavoring to capture the essence and spirit of "Cantares de Cíbola," is to point out the abundance of themes. They run the gamut from God's magical creation of nature in "The Desert Artist," unlimited human largesse in "A Poet's House," the endurance of perpetual faith in "The

Deserted Mission," to youth's innocence or arrogance, as depicted in "Ballad of a Fiddler."

Throughout "Cantares de Cíbola," Fray Angélico avails himself of the New Mexico landscape, from the desert's sierras, sagebrush, canyons, pine trees, junipers, and mesas, to its people, among them the Pueblo Indians and the Navajo, to its landmarks—Mother Nature's wonderland—like Ácoma (the Sky City) and Shiprock. Upon each entity, singularly and collectively, he places poetic expressions, using images, symbols, and metaphors that create a colorful mosaic, resembling a multicolored tapestry that palpitates with life while depicting past as well as present.

While "Cantares de Cíbola" is quite varied in its diversity of themes, "Cantares de María," the second installment of poems in *Cantares: Canticles and Poems of Youth—1925–1932,* deals specifically with what can be called *literatura mariana,* or Marian literature related to the Virgin Mary. This type of literature was popularized during the Middle Ages in Spain by the religious poet Gonzalo de Berceo (1195?–1265?) who wrote "Milagros de Nuestra Señora ("Miracles of the Virgin Mary"). Fray Angélico's "Cantares de María," dedicated to the Virgin Mary, are exclusively religious in content, and, with the exception of one or two poems, constitute a corpus of Marian literature that brings to mind Berceo himself. Regardless of the multiplicity of sobriquets, such as the Lady of the Snows, a Lady Beautiful, the Sweet Mother of the Franciscans, My Lady, the Priestess, La Conquistadora, La Virgen de Guadalupe, or just plain Mother or Mary, the Virgin Mother is portrayed employing different poetic images. Christian lullabies, while she sings "gently and slow," and shepherds "breathe softly the length of their flutes, and angels play carols on viols and lutes," epitomize Fray Angélico's lyrical beauty. He shows us, moreover, that the Virgin Mary's love between her and Jesus, like that of all mothers and sons, is all-encompassing and transcendental, as we can see in "Our Lady's First Communion" when he says:

She kneels as when the Angel came,
Long years before, and called her name.
Her lonely breast no longer grieves
But gently with all heaven heaves,
For Mother's heart is happiest when
Her loving Son comes home again.[10]

But veneration of the Virgin Mary comes not only from the poet's pen; it also emanates from the artist's brush as well. For example, a so-called "quiet" painting by a master like Murillo, in Fray Angélico's estimation, says more than words in describing the Virgin Mary's beauty. The incomparable magnificence of Murillo's masterpiece *The Immaculate Conception,* with its "glorious tones" and majestic crown as her tresses float "on a sea of mist," as Fray Angélico describes it, is memorable indeed.

The dove, rainbow, crescent moon, golden straw, white clouds, singing birds, and fluttering swallows, coupled with lilies and roses and a host of additional images, all appear to rest contentedly, as if on a multicolored quilt of joy and happiness. The Virgin Mary, like a translucent image, seems to spring forth and land on this beautiful quilt, thus coalescing into unmatched splendor, elegance and love. In the mien, a reader feels enveloped, if not draped, by Fray Angélico's exquisite imagery of the Virgin Mary. Reading his Marian poems in absolute solitude evokes a feeling of serenity, solace, and peace of mind.

"Cantares Franciscanos," like "Cantares de María," is devoted to one specific theme—the Franciscan friars. Fray Angélico's inspiration to become a member of the mendicant order stems from his boyhood days in San Diego. Later on, while back in Mora, New Mexico, Fray Angélico learned of the Franciscans' presence in his native state. His fondness for Saint Francis and his order is laid out in "Cantares Franciscanos" using an array of poetical images and forms.

The first poem, "Brown Shadow," opens fittingly with typical Fray Angélico lyricism—a brown shadow tantalizingly plays hide and seek with the spire of the abbey and its projected cross on the lawn. Such an image suggests at the very least that its silhouette is perhaps none other than St. Francis praying. All of the proper ingredients—shadow, spire, window, lawn, song, lyre—come into play in unparalleled musical fashion. Like a symphony in perfect harmony, "the brown shadow of the spire of an abbey on the grass" provides the harmonious imaginary sounds that can only be superseded or surpassed in heaven or paradise.

Virtually every single poem in "Cantares Franciscanos" serves as a chant (canto) or sweet canticle (cántico), an ode of sorts, bestowed upon Saint Francis of Assis. His benevolence and good deeds and the inspiration he invoked upon his protégés or followers throughout time are made manifest. Fray Angélico's praise and adulation of Saint Francis are taken to lofty heights in "Franciscan Poet," for it is he in particular who is capable of extricating or lifting oneself from the doldrums of dejection, as tolerance and forgiveness ultimately reign supreme:

Be a poet like your Father
Toiling not or earthly years;
Sing your lyrics in your sorrow,
Write your poems with your tears.

Then appear before the Master,
Fearing neither woe nor curse,
For the Book of Life will open
And reveal a Book of Verse. (*Cantares*)

Yet not every poem is serious either in intent, purpose, or attitude. Fray Angélico, as we have witnessed before, tends to indulge in humor and consequently allows for levity to surface from time to time as part of his persona. "Silly Lyric" is a case in point; it is a playful exchange between Saint Francis and the swallows, one of Fray Angélico's favorite birds:

Swallow, lovely swallow, called
St. Francis to a swallow,

. . . .

So they sang until the swallow
Fell asleep like any swallow,
While the saint, like any fellow,
Went and found himself a pillow
'Neath a willow on the hill. (*Cantares*)

Throughout all of the Franciscan poetry, no single verse, stanza, or poem stands out more vividly in Fray Angélico's repertoire than "Little Poor Man to Little Boy Blue." His call to join the humble Franciscan Order comes across in simple and straightforward language:

Lay aside the blue jeans, Little Boy Blue!
For richer garments are waiting for you.
Now, put on my brown,
The hood and the gown.
And the girdle Big Brother of Padua knew.
Lay aside the blue jeans, Little
Boy Blue. (*Cantares*)

As if to utter the final words to a closing chapter, Fray Angélico offers us his last poem in "Cantares Franciscanos," "The Barefoot Boy." It comprises not only the vision of a young boy in becoming a Franciscan, perhaps a reflection of his own childhood aspiration, but an inkling of a dream come true. Both perspectives are interwoven in cogent and modest terms:

The barefoot boy is gone from home,
But will come back anon;
And though he sing of silver shoon,
He'll come with sandals on. (*Cantares*)

This last poem, coupled with "Brown Shadow," the first one discussed under "Cantares Franciscanos, completes a cycle in Fray Angélico's adulation of Saint Francis and his fellow Franciscan brethren. His poetics, even in clear and uncluttered lexicon, have a magical and musical way of their own that at times is even unpredictable.

"Cantares Varios," the final repertoire of poems (a total of seventy-four) brought together in *Cantares: Canticles and Poems of Youth—1925–1932*, represent, as the title clearly suggests, a potpourri of themes as varied as Fray Angélico's creative adeptness. As a matter of fact, his poetic talent mirrors the diversification of themes that he tackles in this last corpus of poetry. The topics cover a melodic and joyful poetry that surges forth like magic in multi-colors through wind and string instruments in "Canticle of the Rainbow," the opening poem, to more solemn overtures of the love for Christ expressed in a lyrical, ascetic, and quasi-mystical mode in the last poem, "All for Love."

In between these poems' two different yet seemingly reconcilable worlds rests a myriad of delightful verses likely to warm even the cold-hearted. Without delving into an in-depth study of Fray Angélico's poems, the most pragmatic approach for appreciating his poetic finesse in "Cantares Varios" in particular, and his poetics in general, is to sit down and leisurely read this last collection from beginning to end. In doing so, the reader gets an unforgettable experience replete with highs and lows, joys and sorrow, nature's wonders, resplendent colors, faith, love, and charity, and other topics not likely to be erased from memory overnight.

Many of his poems are naturally religious in content, but also unforgettable are "The Little Flower," a beautiful garden turned paradise, and "To a Little Orphan Girl," joy and sorrow coalescing into a moment of happiness as we see here:

> Sometimes, when it is dark, your face comes up,
> Your eyes like water in a sapphire cup,

Searching my soul the way our guardian angels do.
And then I feel a little glad
That golden hearts have closed about and gilded you,
And somewhat sad.[11]

But one of the most sobering poems in "Cantares Varios" is "First Poem." In it we see life's fleeting journey on this earth—the fugacity of time—analogous to a fresh flower today and "faded and torn" tomorrow—the brevity of beauty—as "youth's graces and charms" come to a close at dusk, thus bringing life to an abrupt end. This poem is suggestive of the popular medieval concept in Europe of the *ubi sunt,* made famous in Spain by Jorge Manrique (1440?–1479) in his poem *Coplas por la muerte de su padre,* an elegy written upon the death of his father.

From beginning to end, *Cantares: Canticles and Poems of Youth—1925–1932* is a kaleidoscope of colors, feelings, and emotions spread across a poetic blanket that raises the level of idyllic imagery to universal proportions. Lest we forget and are unduly critical because of his style, tone, or attitude, Fray Angélico's poetry, was written when he was a young boy during the 1920s and early 1930s. By and large, the reader will find his poems upbeat and cheerful, for they often glitter with beaming colors and engaging metaphors that tremble like stars on a dark, serene sky. The ultimate feeling is one of tranquility that simply leaves readers in a soothing and pleasant mood.

Nasario García
New Mexico Highlands University

Notes

[1]Fray Angélico Chávez, "Fray Angélico Chávez: Main Biographical & Literary Points," to Nasario García, 27 January 1993. Henceforth Fray Angélico.

[2]Antonio (Tony) Chávez letter to Nasario García, 8 October 1999. Henceforth Antonio Chávez.

[3]Tom E. Chávez, Interview by Nasario García, 26 August 1999, Santa Fe, NM. Henceforth Tom E. Chávez.

[4]Santa Teresa de Jesús, "I Die Because I Do Not Die," eds. Seymour Resnick and Jeanne Pasmantier, trans. E. Allison Peers, *An Anthology of Spanish Literature in English Translation* (New York: Frederick Ungar Publishing Co, 1958), 185.

[5]Fray Angélico Chávez, *Clothed With the Sun* (Santa Fe: Writer's Editions, Inc., 1939), 29. "I Vowed" also appears in *Cantares: Canticles and Poems of Youth—1925–1932*.

[6]Antonio Chávez, included this poem of Fray Angélico's in his August 26, 1999, letter to me.

[7]Tom E. Chávez to Nasario García, 23 January 2000.

[8]Fray Angélico. While stationed at Camp Chaffee, Arkansas (1943–1944), he drove to Little Rock to visit John Gould Fletcher at his family's estate. He died a short time after Fray Angélico's visit.

[9]"Cantares," *Cantares: Canticles and Poems of Youth—1925–1932*. Subsequent listings will appear as *Cantares*.

[10]"Our Lady's First Communion," "*The Provincial Chronicle of St. John Baptist Province*, vol. 4 (April 1932), 126.

[11]"To a Little Orphan Girl," *St. Anthony Messenger*, vol. 42 (November 1934), 371.

Statue of Fray Angélico Chávez in front of the Fray Angélico Chávez Library and Photographic Archives, 1997. Courtesy of Tom Chávez, Collections of the Palace of the Governors.

Cantares de Cíbola

Cantares

I weave a lariat of words
To catch the Winged Horse;
And with the cry of many birds
It whistles in its course.

But when my song is o'er, I fear
I caught no horse with wings:
For there's no Muse's lyre here—
It is the rope that sings.

The Desert Artist

His colors are the turquoise blue
And the hues which the cliffs perspire;
Deep purples, yellows — orange, too,
And a red like a hogan's fire.

The mesa rim,
His palette trim,
At sunset holds his color stain.
He paints a frieze
Which no one sees
With a sage-brush dipped in rain.

I see the brush and the palette trim,
When the sun-bird downward flees,
But I never saw His Hand nor Him,
And His canvas no one sees.

When mesa rim,
His palette trim,
At sunset shines for me in vain,

I hope to view
That scene He drew
With a sage-brush dipped in rain.

Pegasus

O winged steed, 'tis dawning soon,
A purple cloud floats o'er me here,
And 'neath it swings the silver moon,
A crescent on an Indian's ear.
Come, let me see your soaring form,
And watch your light hoofs rise and sink,
Like foamy crests on sea that storm
At the day-moon's silver wink.
Who calls below my window ledge?
Bellerophon, of you how good,
To bring your steed of silver sedge
With his wings of cedar wood:
Come, brother, drive your burro thus;
I'll buy your firewood to-day . . .
What forms you take, O Pegasus —
A Winged Horse, you came my way.

The Paintings

After Japanese Patterns

What harmonies does Nature show,
Yet scarce would call them one—
The sunset-tinted mountain snow,
The sierra-painting sun.

Grayish silver of the desert sage,
Not woe you give me, but a happy thought:
I found a silver song in every page
Of every gray and gloomy book I bought.

How fresh and new the sierras in the rain,
Just when the Maytime sun is shining, too;
What showers fall, each drop half-light, half-dew!
So have my smiles not sipped my tears in vain.

I wandered down the cedared hill
And found white crosses—unaware,
I counted them and then stood still —
I counted one that was not there.

A Poet's House

A pagan house without sees the wind,
Of Indian pueblo clay.
A heathen house within feeds the mind
With treasures from Cathay.
Yet, in that house one good and kind
Pours forth a soothing lay,
Where neither East nor West I find:
Just song—the human way.

Cinquains to the Padre

To W.B. [Witter Bynner]

Ácoma

Padre,
Transfigured in
The lofty solitude of the mesa
Silhouetted on the moon.

Stone Rainbow

Iris
Of the rainless spaces,
Finder at the stone-rainbow's foot

Of the pot
Of gold.

Sangre de Cristo

Pine trees
Above the timber-line,
Without the comfort of the valley—
But closer to
The sky.

Shiprock

Seaman
Of the desert galley
On the Spanish sandy main,
Sent by the Master of the boat
On Galilee.

The Southwest

Padre,
Motif of the landscape,
Sunlight on the Pueblo and the Villa:
Like the Mission, brown and old—
Still there.

I Wondered and I Asked Myself

I wondered and I asked myself:
What does the poet gain
By songs of airy nothingness
And turquoise skies?
And I could not answer myself,
And myself then asked of me:
Why is the silver sage,

Which like a broom
Sweeps the sky all summer,
Tipped now in autumn
With dust of gold?

The Painting Poet

I plucked a feather with a cactus drill
From the gray wing of a thrush;
One side I sharpened to a poet's quill,
The other end, a painter's brush.

I paint the sage upon the shady ground
With pigment-words of silver-jades,
And then I turn my wonder-pen around
And with it add the purple shades.

"Foreign" New Mexico

Before the galleys of the roving Norn
Had slipped their anchors by a western world;
Before the ancient Pilgrim Father fell
Upon his knees on famous Plymouth Rock;
There was a Land, a Race, a Cult, a Faith,
Within the greatest nation of this earth
Whose seed, just then, not even had been sown.

Before the foreign ore from alien mines
Had poured into this melting pot of ours;
Just when our glorious flag existed high
Upon the starry skies, and spangled snows
And red wild blossoms-far from dreams of men,
This was a kingdom.

Full three centuries
Have flown since the Conquistadores came,
Brave armored soldiery, the golden might
That then was Spain; brown-robed, rope-girted [sic] souls,
Pure jewels of their land, whose every life
Draws forth the admiration of all men.
They came, they saw, they conquered all—but death;
Yet, left upon their path a heritage.
One left his flesh and blood, the other gave
His Cross and life, that both live on in peace.
Christened with the Padre's martyr-blood,
The child of the Conquistador grew on
And clung to every priestless mission wall,
Through centuries forgotten and unsung.

Isolated, sunk within a sea
Of dream-oblivion, this Atlantis lay,
Unknown, until the distant seed was sown
That grew and spread its tender branches west,
Encircling all this treasure, land and race,
And making all its own.

Behold, therefore,
Ye hosts of steely metal, mighty girders
Of our grand, sky-seeking edifice;
Behold, thou alien ore re-melted here
Within the mighty cauldron, see and think!
Let justice judge this land, untainted thus
By even kindred neighbors. See the Spain
Of centuries agone, untouched withal
By e'en her distant mother. See the State
Least foreign to our glorious country now—
New Mexico, the eldest, yet—most young!

On the Alameda

The Alameda leans against the evening
Silhouetted.

That grove beside the river
Is a mosque,
That weeping willow
Is the dome of jade,
Those poplars are the slender minarets.
I am walking through Arabia,
Alone.

The Angelus chimes from the Cathedral,
And I am walking home
With you.

Roses

God gave to me a rose to kiss,
A bursting, blushing rose,
Still, I was not content;
He pressed a cactus to your lips:
You looked at Him and smiled—
You gave to God a rose to kiss.

Mountain Padres

A prior am I. My friary
Stands where it is not seen
By blinded eyes that cannot see
A singing sunset sheen
Nor psalters in an aspen tree
Or a chanting evergreen.

And every day my monks appear
On granite stalls and wide
Singing their songs for God to hear;
From morn till even-tide
They stand enchoired, tier on tier,
Upon the mountainside.

No monks were e'er so much alone
In prayerful whispering,
As trees that in their stalls have grown;
What psalms the pines can sing,
As if for ages they have known
That God is listening!

Night in the Canyon

A purple velvet, spacious, grand,
    Then a dash of silver shine;
The aspens, each a sterling wand,
    Wave their leaves of argentine.

City of Saint Francis

City Beautiful and Oldest,
City Different and Strange,
Santa Fe, City Franciscan—
Assisi thou, without a change!

West? The West, what does it matter,
Distant from a distant East?
What St. Francis made Assisi
That he makes of thee, at least.

Sons of Francis made thy glory
With their blood, so we are told;

Things Franciscan are of Francis,
Francis gilt thee with his gold.

See the lovely Umbrian woodlands,
Forests that can never change,
Stepping gracefully to heaven
Up Sangre de Cristo range.

Ere his Sun Hymn had been chanted,
Did he, turning to the west,
See that fan of rays and rainbows
Spread to view on Jémez' crest?

Sun Hymn? Why, his dear La Verna
Was the kingly Monte Sol!
And the Seraph—Sun of Zia
Blazoned on a golden scroll!

Santa Fe, City Franciscan,
Pride thyself of such a name,
For thy glories are Assisi's
Different, yet all the same.

A Burro on the Plaza

Ungrateful fools, you laugh at me:
A load of wood is nothing new.
One whom I often gladly bore
Was loaded also—and for you!

Santa Fe Skyline

Like a blue-veined marble altar rise the sierras,
Still covered with an altar-cloth of snow;

While the facing sunset stains the altar-linen
With blood, and eastern stars like candles glow.

Right at the altar's foot the flat-roofed houses huddle
In broken order, whitish, grey, and browned,
Like the cowled and prostrate forms of long-dead Padres
Kissing with tenderness the holy ground.

The Deserted Mission

She stands alone between the canyon walls,
Roofless, weatherworn, 'mid graves erased.
The Door is open where adorers gazed
Three hundred years ago. No blessing falls
On lonely worshippers in faded shawls.
The Royal Arms lie shattered on the floor;
The "Cross and Arms" still hang above the door,
Awaiting help beyond the canyon's halls.

And yet, without a guardian does she stay,
With roofless walls, the sands that ages toss;
O ye who toil for Holy Church to-day,
Regard this martyrs' monument a loss?
A hopeless, priestless, roofless chapel?—Nay!
The Chancel is not broken, nor the Cross!

My Country

Long ago saw the rovers Hellenic
A land by the sunset bar,
Which they called in their language "Hesperia",
The home of the evening star.

Her the legions of conquering Romans
"Hispania" they named again;

And the world recognized through the ages
The beauty and might of Spain.

Then the Padres joined hands with the angels
And far to the sunset glow
Carried part of the lovely "España"
And called her "New Mexico."

The Archbishop's Garden

Santa Fe

Pink hollyhocks and juniper tops and
a silvery fountain spray,
Long shady walks where the willow tear
drops and a figure in silver-gray;
A wall of adobe too high for us,
A hedge of adobe that hides from us
Pink hollyhocks and juniper tops, made
lovely for others to spy;
But you and I must gaze and sigh and
pass them by.

Low creak the slow spokes with the
weight of wheels,
With the patter of a thousand wooden heels.
The Alameda wakes, as o'er it crawls
A covered wagon by the garden walls,
With chile, melons, apricots and pears,
With hand-carved wooden santos, chests and chairs.

Isidro halts his team aside the dreamy street
And, kneeling on the lofty wagon seat,
Peeps over the adobe wall to see
The beauties hidden both from you and me—

Then moves away contented with his wares
Of chile, peaches, apricots and pears.

Pink hollyhocks and juniper tops and
  a silvery fountain spray,
Long shady walks where the willow tear
  drops and a figure in silver-gray;
  A wall of adobe too high for us,
  A hedge of adobe that hides from us
Pink hollyhocks and juniper tops, made
  lovely for others to spy;
But you and I must gaze and sigh and pass them by.

Cross of the Friar-Martyrs

One day at eve I climbed the scarlet mound
Where stood the holy goal I sought,
And when I came upon the hallowed ground,
I saw no Martyrs' Cross, I thought.

I knelt and prayed with sorrow keen and deep:
There stood against the night
With outstretched arms over the city's sleep—
A friar bathed in light.

Dawn at the Missions

"Ya viene el Alba . . ."

Now comes the dawn o'er poppied lawn
  And breaks the glorious day.
With joyous ring "Hail Mary" sing,
  And to our Mother pray.
The Padre's song echoes among
  The dripping weeping willows;

Still wet with dew the dovelets coo
    Among their leafy pillows.
Their clear notes falling
        In tune with the fountain
    Bring voices calling
        With joy from the mountain,
"Most Beautiful Queen of the Heavens!"

Now comes the dawn, the night is gone,
    Aurora breaks the day.
Both gallant Don and humble peon
    To Mary chant and pray.
The Mistress tells her beads; now wells
    With tears the Padre's lay,
For one unseen sings to his Queen
    The Franciscan roundelay.

    Ramona sings,
        And Heaven's throng
    With morning brings
        Love to her song—
"Most beautiful Queen of the Heavens!"

Now comes the dawn o'er poppied lawn
    And breaks the glorious day.
With joyous ring "Hail Mary" sing,
    And to our Mother pray.
Now fled the days, and dead the ways,
    When dawn was welcomed so;
When soul of Spain with birds' refrain
    First watched the morning glow.
        What gladness rang,
            That joyous day,

When people sang
That roundelay,
"Most beautiful Queen of the Heavens!"

Dust

Into the sun-broiled daze
That blurred the gray sage nigh
A yellow clouded haze
Upon the desert seemed to fly.
Before my weary gaze,
In woolly foam, a flock of sheep came flowing,
And with its surging drowned the sky
In swirling dust, a cloudlet, cloud-ward going.

Enchanting desert dust,
But dust you are, like me;
For turn to dust I must
And lie beneath a dusty sea.
No sweeping desert gust
Shall heave that arid tide with all its trying;
Yet, when the fateful day shall be,
A Lamb will raise a cloudlet, cloud-ward flying.

Navajo

The Navajo is tall,
Steep like a canyon wall;
The Navajo lives far,
Much like a roaming star.
But, be he kingly high,
He cannot reach the sky,
And feeble is his light,
Engulfed in blackest night.

Now, who will lead him near,
Bring light to slavish fear,
And show to him how high
Is, after all, the sky?

It is the patience of love
It is the generous hand—
The soul that soars above
For light to understand.

The Mission Guadalupe

The Mission Guadalupe
Is like a smoke-mist pueblo kiva
In the morning.

The pink-painted dawn-priest
Comes out upon the roof
With a ruby lamp.
He lights it on the rising sun—
And I follow him
Into the smoke-mist kiva.

Wine of the vine and grain of the plain
Are on the sacrificial stone
Alone . . .
The ruby lamp dries up the dark—
And I see the Beloved.

At night the Guadalupe
Is like my heart, without windows,
But it burns a ruby lamp.

A Song of the Padre

"The wild vines are loaded with grapes and
the roses are like the roses of Castile."
—Letter of Fr. Serra.

I love it when the sunset drapes
My desert garden with a charm I feel,
While to those red and purple shapes
My old bells faintly peal:
The vines are loaded all with grapes,
And the roses are the roses of Castile.

Flown are my first evenings of sadness,
Tuned are the peals that made me feel so sad;
Red and purple are now hues of gladness,
And those ancient bells chime but to make me glad . . .
Mine was a work of lonesome sorrow,
Far from the breath of kin, from home's romance,
Now must I wait each day that each to-morrow
Bring me each evening that enlightens me and chants:

I love it when the sunset drapes
My desert garden with a charm I feel,
While to those red and purple shapes
My old bells faintly peal:
The vines are loaded all with grapes
And the roses are the roses of Castile.

The Worshippers

God clasped the hand of Sister Life with mine
And bade me roam His happy world with her,
To offer sacrifice and raise His Sign
Among the cedar, sage, and juniper;

Then, promised us His Home and raised a pine
That pointed to our future temple there.

Our temple is the country we call home,
A sanctuary 'neath a boundless dome,
Where Nature prays, fresh from His Wonder-Hand,
In tumbling monuments of stone and sand.
Our sexton is the wind, the thunderman,
Who carves our altars on the mesa's breast,
And makes his mighty organ's rumblings span
The desert's mammoth piles from crest to crest.
A Padre worships, vapors skyward roll:
I am the priest, my censer is my soul.

With purple cedar berries, mountain myrrh,
Perfumed within the sage's fragrant soul,
Life grinds the ruby resin of the fir
Then, pounds her incense in a turquoise bowl.

She pours it slowly in my censer fires,
Grain by grain in measured ecstasy,
And, as the opal smoke in snake-like spires
Curls upward through the azure vaults above,
I know her Father—Father, too, for me—
Is pleased and smiles upon our gift of love.

Some day an angel, death, will come for her,
But, with her gone, my self must follow, too;
And, if my heart is gone, what comforter
Will hold me from the loving joy I knew?
Life is mine, my own to keep fore'er,
For, when He placed her spotless hand in mine,
He promised us His Home and raised a pine
That pointed to our future temple there.

Fray Serra

With poppy seeds he strewed his way;
And forth there sprang a golden trail
And marked his footprints for to-day.

When, after gazing o'er the bay,
He knew he yearned to no avail,
With poppy seeds he strewed his way.

And, as he stopped to rest and pray,
Each bloom became a golden nail
And marked his footprints for to-day.

From Carmel on, to San Luis Rey,
To link a chain that would not fail
With poppy seeds he strewed his way.

San Diego, back to Monterey,
They flooded in a golden gale
And marked his footprints for to-day.

Old California, fresh and gay,
And all her Missions chime the tale:
With poppy seeds he strewed his way,
And marked his footprints for to-day.

A Litany of Pueblos

San Gerónimo de Taos

St. Jerome:
Like your Bethlehem
The terraces of Taos wave up and down;
With the knowledge of unwritten Vulgates,

Like your lion,
The tawny people frown—
Pray for us.

San Juan de los Caballeros

St. John:
Here is the pueblo
Where came the Padre first with the Cavalier,
Whose glamour is a memory of faded blood,
A desert Patmos to Sangre de Cristo near—
Pray for us.

Santa Clara

St. Clare:
Like bright-hued Saracens
Who fell before the Host you bore,
On Corpus Christi day these people fall,
But to adore—
Pray for us.

San Ildefonso

St. Ildephonse:
Your primatial Toledo
Sleeps brown and broken by the Río Grande;
Behold your great cathedral,
Or is it the Black Mesa, steep and sandy?
Pray for us.

San Buenaventura de Cochití

St. Bonaventure:
Lowly Francis reigns
In the cathedral at Santa Fe,
While you, Lord Cardinal, throned on adobe,
Hold silent council with chiefs that passed away—
Pray for us.

Santo Domingo

St. Dominic:
No torch of yours
Flares in the mouths of dogs, Coyote-tame;
Nor heretics are these brown inquisitive faces,
But pagans still, though calling on His Name—
Pray for us.

San Felipe

St. Philip:
Can aught of good come out of Nazareth?
Or out of San Felipe? Or the other Missions?
This much, that God is praised with fervent breath—
Pray for us.

In the Arms of the Pine Tree

I

In the arms of the pine tree kneeling lonely on the mountain,
When the moon comes out to meet me
    in the middle of the sky,

I look down upon the valley, on two willows by a fountain,
And the wind breathes me the echo of
a far and yearning sigh.

II

In the cool of the fountain, in
whose depths the willows' tresses
Dip their olive-green reflections, I
once knew the nestling's bliss;
In their intertwining branches,
down their emerald caresses,
I had stooped to childhood's fountain
and received a crystal kiss.

III

But one night I saw a pine tree in
the deepness of its streaming,
As though talking to the moon that
in the water seemed to flow,
And I winged me to the mountain
where the silver moon was beaming,
And I left the weeping willows in
the valley depths below.

IV

In the arms of the pine tree kneeling
lonely on the mountain,
I look down upon the willows that in
warming moonbeams swoon;
Silence . . . hear: a whisper cometh
with the sweetness of the fountain,

"Find us happy by the moonlight, son,
—we see you on the moon."

Ácoma

Why, is this not the temple, God-endowed,
That Moses might have built on Sinai's height?
Or stands it here to tempt the eagle's flight
With nesting space of which it can be proud?
Perhaps it is the moormast of a cloud,
Or else a beacon for the noon-day light!—
And yet, a Padre, with his Lord's foresight,
Built all this on a rock, alone, unbowed.
Cathedral of the White-Rock-People, hail!
Christ's Rock's lone picture on this continent,
Bound to the earth with stone unknown to fail,
Yet comrade to the turquoise firmament.
Live on, live on, through sun and rain and gale,
The redman's pride, Franciscan monument.

Pecos Ruins

We were a nation once, firm in our trust
That ever would our children's children dwell
Among these pines and cedars; but we fell
By slow degrees to earth, as all men must,
The redman back into the red, red dust.
One thing remains: the walls we loved so well,
Wherein we learned of life to come—they tell
Of this our faith, with every passing gust.
Faithful Guardian of a Grateful Dead!
For you alone tell where our houses stood;
And only you remain to pray and shed
A tear, as true surviving kinsmen should.

You are the tomb above our silent bed,
The marker o'er our heads, your cross of wood.

A Dance in Cochití

Behold the dancers, like a rusty chain,
Heave slowly in a brown unbroken line,
Before a saint within his leafy shrine,
The tasseled monarch of a strange domain.
Behold the dancers, how they call the rain
With fox-skins, rattles, and with sprays of pine,
All pagan symbols of the sly's white wine,—
A prayer for plenty at a Christian fane.
St. Bonaventure, Lord of Cochití,
O brown-robed Padre of Red-Hat-with-Tassels!
Make every tassel of the corn to see
The roof-tops of your brown adobe castles.
O Father, rain! The Rain! Rain let it be—
The sign between a Chieftain and his Vassals!

Cíbola's Cathedral

Nature built cathedrals before man;
Clouds push up Quiviran heavens, dome on dome,
Like the air-embracing vault of St. Sophia,
Or loom immobile for a span
While sage-strewn deserts gaze on Rome;
And then again Sevilla
In red-ribbed Moorish arches flashes on the western sky;
While San Mateo's pines in Gothic naves fly rocket-high,
No transept quite alone,
But Durham piled on Notre Dame,
Amiens on Lincoln, Rheims on tall Cologne . . .
But none of these is Ácoma—a far cry
From trees in stone,

Or domed cloud-foam,
Or sunset arabesques of Spain;
For, besides the clouds and sun and forest trees,
God placed the mesas on the plain,
And Ácoma is one of these—
A mesa made by man.

Wings of Death

There is no sign of Cicuyé,
Black spots crawl on the sky.
Fray Luis for days has lost his way
And knows he now will die.

Oh, had he stayed with Padre Juan,
He too would now be dead,
Killed by the Tiguas—not alone
To die of thirst instead.

But Padre Juan had given word
For Luis to leave Tigüez:
The gospel that the Tiguas heard
Must sound in Cicuyé.

And Luis, obedient to the last,
Crawls 'neath a heartless sun,
And whispers as he sinks down fast,
"God's holy Will be done."

He crumples on the baking sands,
Wings flutter overhead;
He smiles: "Unto the rightful hands
"This booty of the dead."

No war of wings follows his moans,
But each pair takes its toll—
The vultures swoop to pick his bones,
The angels lift his soul.

Saint Michael's Window

The broad façade of that tall precipice
Bears up a mammoth circle, gaping high,
Carved by the wind and rain and rending ice,
And fitted with a flawless pane of sky.

What ancient wonders go you out to view
In moldy minster piles of lands abroad,
When here a bit of heaven is smiling through
A window by the sculptor-men of God!

Go with God

He passed me at the corner,
Tapping his rod,
Nor paused to beg an alms,
Which I deemed odd.

For, having heard my voice,
He dared not ask,
Sensing, perhaps, in youth
A futile task.

I had an only coin,
My own to spend;
I stopped and thought and stepped
Around the bend.

"For love of God and you,
My countryman—"

I pressed it in his palm,
  And turned and ran.

He stood there rapt in wonder,
  Tapping his rod.
"Go with God!" he cried—
  I went with God.

Parable

When the sun sits down
  at the mesa's ledge
And the purpling clouds
  hang all around,
I think of Dives
  at his table's edge,
Ruddy and round and
  in purple gowned.

Then some golden crumbs
  off the mesa's rim
Fall toward a pine
  at the mesa's foot—
A scraggly Lazarus,
  scarred of limb,
And coyotes digging
  at its root.

Ballad of a Fiddler

From San José, old people say,
A youthful fiddler came to town,
Who in the patios used to play—
While youths and maidens danced and kissed,
Or threw their souls away.

He played of knights whose hearts were strong,
Because their thoughts and deeds were pure;
Of ladies fair who knew no wrong,
Nor pledged their lilies for a weed
During a minstrel's song.

Love could no better music find
Than his, whose large and staring eyes
The young romancers did not mind:
The while he played, they played their hearts,
Knowing that he was blind.

To San José, there finally
Returned the fiddler who was blind;
And all did wonder mightily,
Because he loudly thanked the Lord
That he could see.

Tango

I hear the wind upon my casement,
drumming on my window pane
A lilting wild fandango;
And he calls me to the moonlight,
by the poplar-pillared lane,
Singing of enchanting ballads that the river mourns in vain,
Singing of a scene of beauty that it cannot see again
Singing of the charming tango.

And I walk into the garden by the old adobe wall,
Stepping to the wild fandango;
There I hear the east wind whisper
of the canyon's dancing hall,
Pointing to Sangre de Cristo,
where the midnight golden ball

Beams upon the canyon which he calls
the winged horse's stall,
Beams upon the forest tango.

There's a tango, there's a tango
Where the wind and river listen;
And they dance a wild fandango
Where the forest colors glisten.

Hear the low-complaining river,
How he murmurs through in vain,
For he must flow down forever
And not see that scene again.

But 'tis I, the wind, who's happy,
for I roam the world at will,
Singing ever the fandango.
With my gentle humming breath
I make the forest music trill,
While the dancers of the canyon sway
and shudder, wave and thrill,
As my mellow, merry murmurs drown the
all-complaining rill—
Yes, I have seen the tango.

The steel strings strum to the tripping thrum
Of the castanets and slippers as they go and come;
To their rapping, tapping clapping and
their measured mellow drum,
For there's swaying dreamy rhythm with
the sharp staccato from
The Great Salon of Night in the Canyon.

The turquoised-tinseled junipers in waving
blurs wave to the firs,

The castanetting conifers re-echo thru the canyon.
The jaded spruce and cedar swoon and
lean their heads upon the moon,
While moonlight floods the trees with
noon within the dreamy canyon.

They've hung the lantern on the night,
a golden light, Diana's light,
And gilt the valley golden bright
within the forest canyon.
Confetti flakes and streamers gay
are sparkling on the Milky Way
And twinkling over Santa Fe
with silver from the canyon.

The aspens lift their hems of jade and
twinkling discs of silver braid,
And with their snowy bare legs wade the river in the canyon.
Above the hall's mosaic stones the graceful
pine tree shakes her cones
And dances to the forest tones, castanetting
through the canyon.

The steel strings strum to the tripping thrum
Of the castanets and slippers as they go and come,
To their rapping, tapping clapping and
their measured mellow drum,
For there's swaying dreamy rhythm with
the sharp staccato from
The Great Salon of Night in the Canyon.

I have seen the people dancing for the rain in Cochití,
Saw them in Santo Domingo;
Saw the tireless, springing pumping of
the feather-banded knee

And the shaking fox-skin swinging to its dull monotony;
Saw the many, many dancers in a heaving umber sea,
    But this was not a tango.

Santa Clara, where the pottery is black like bowling balls,
    Has her yearly fandango;
There the dancers slowly amble, as the
    drum-beat deeply falls,
With the sway of bobbing bison heads and
    living deerskin dolls,
With the dipping of the antlers as the line in circles crawls—
    Yet, this is not a tango.

Far upon the lofty Moqui you might hear
    some day, by chance,
    A primitive fandango;
You will feel the measured drum-beats
    and the steady thudding prance,
As the priests, with snakes mouth-laden,
    in a squirming train advance,
Writhing, rattling to the rhythm of the
    chanting and the dance,
    Still, this is not a tango.

Long ago I bore a melody upon the desert sand;
    It was no gay fandango;
Grey-robed Padres plodded onward with a
    Cross upon their hand,
Singing, chanting forth a music that
    was solemn, deep, and grand;
And though sweeter, grander music has
    not come upon this land,
    It was no happy tango.

The thirsty throstle whistles on the rustling thistle stocks
    A harsh and thin fandango;
And the gray-green little lizards leap
    and dart among the rocks,
Through the sheaves of silver sagebrush
    and the golden grassy shocks,
While the pink bells ring in rhythm
    on the swinging hollyhocks—
    But this is not a tango.

You have heard the glad, loud clapping
    of the chuckling castanets
    In a Fiesta-time fandango;
You have seen the dancing fingers step
    the strings upon the frets,
With a pair of lightning lashes 'neath
    the trembling tambourettes
Lightly flashing playful messages of
    mutual loves and threats—
    Yes, this they called a tango.

You have seen he ancient Villa dressed in red and yellow-gold
    For the Fiesta-time fandango;
And have seen me blow mantillas that the señoritas hold,
Like the wind-swept colored butterflies
        before the breezes bold,
Fluttering o'er scarlet tulips on a field of marigold—
    You thought it was a tango.

    There's a tango, there's a tango
    Where the wind and river listen;
    And they dance a wild fandango
    Where the forest colors glisten.

Hear the low-complaining river,
How he murmurs through in vain,
For he must flow down forever
And not see that scene again.

But 'tis I, the wind, who's happy, for
I roam the world at will,
Singing ever the fandango;
Now I hasten to the canyon, for the pines have not their fill,
Nor the wading, white-legged aspens in
the murmuring mountain rill—
See! Around the golden lantern the confetti's flying still
O'er the happy forest tango!

The steel strings strum to the tripping thrum
Of the castanets and slippers as they go and come;
To their tapping, tapping clapping and
their measured mellow drum,
For there's swaying dreamy rhythm with
the sharp staccato from
The Great Salon of Night in the Canyon.

Cantares de María

The Lady of the Snows

Like petals from some garden high,
    Around me fell the snows;
And, as I watched them winging by,
    Behold! a vision rose.
It seemed as if the dancing snow,
    Like roses white and full,
Had clustered deftly, forming, lo!
    —A Lady Beautiful.
Around her beauty snowflakes whirled
    And wove a garment white
That 'round her spun, begemmed and pearled,
    A crystal snow samite.
A snowy veil twirled 'round her head,
    (O face so sweet and mild!)
And on her bosom's tender bed
    Reposed a naked child.

"I am the Lady of the Snows,
    As spotless as my name."
Her voice upon the silence rose,
    As if they were the same.
"I am the Virgin, snowy white,
    The Mother of the Son.
This is not mine, this burden light
    Whose life is just begun—
It is my Son's own gift to thee,
    This naked babe so fair,
Oh, clothe it well and keep it free
    From sinful taint and care.
Take thou this budding winter rose—
    Come, mortal, do not fear:
I am the Lady of the Snows,
    This Babe—the new-born Year."

May Gems

'Neath the sapphire mantle of heaven,
In the emerald freshness of May,
Sang the sunbeam soft to the dewdrops,
As they danced with the gladness of day:
"Ye are all living diamonds and pearls,
Happy jewels in shining array;
Ye are crowns on the grasses and flowers,
Sparkling for the fair Queen of May."

Queen of the Friars Minor

Hail, Virgin Mother! Queen of lowly friars,
List hymns of praise from all that happy throng;
How rich the zeal thy feast to them inspires,
To spread thy name with sermon, deed and song.

'Twas Francis, onc, who sang so well of thee,
Seraphic Saints thy virtues did proclaim.
Duns Scotus taught and proved thy purity,
All Francis' sons did glorify thy name.

From age to age Franciscan tongue and lyre
Have sung and e'er will sing thy dignity;
For us, Sweet Mother, gain this one desire—
Thy love to sing for all eternity.

Our Lady's First Communion

She kneels as when the Angel came,
Long years before, and called her name.
Her lonely breast no longer grieves
But gently with all heaven heaves,
For Mother's heart is happiest when
Her loving Son comes home again.

Sermons in Stones

Into the rock my Lady went
When all the world no pity lent;
And in the stone she gave Him birth,
Who from the stone then blessed the earth.
Upon a rock she fondly laid Him,
And from the storms the rocks did save Him,
And all the stones in silence praised Him,
When into the rock she went.

Into the land of stones she went,
When Herod the heart of Rachel rent.
And near the stones of long-dead kings,
She hid the eternal Lord of Things.
To sleep on the rocks she sweetly lulled Him,
From desert sands the stones did shield Him;
All gentile rocks and stones extolled Him,
When into that land she went.
Back to the rocky hills she came,
When death the cruel king o'er came,
And there among the rocks He played,
And blessed the stones that He had made.
The brook's smooth pebbles were marbles for Him,
The slates on the hillocks were tablets for Him,
The rocks and the stones were all friends to Him,
When back to the hills she came.

To the top of the rock my Saviour went,
By a cross His weary Body bent.
And on a carpet of solid stone,
They raised His painful and bloody Throne.
Those stones on the way had kissed and caressed Him,
That rock to the sight of all sinners did raise Him,

And the stones near the gibbet with pity did face Him,
When up to the rock He went.

Into the rock my Lady went,
With heart transfixed, by woe for spent.
Back to the stone she brought her Son,
From Whom the breath of life was gone.
Back on the stone she tearfully laid Him,
With mute consent the rock received Him,
From contact foul the stone preserved Him,
When into the rock she went.

Out of the rock my Saviour came,
Glorious, immortal, and free from shame.
His temple He built upon a stone,
To Peter, the Rock, he gave the Throne.
With heavenly power endowed by Him,
Daily on the stone the priest does lay Him,
And angels on stone kneel down and adore Him,
Since out of the rock He came.

Dolores

Crowned a Queen on queenly skies
Shines Mary mild with beaming eyes,
While angels pure descend and rise,
Resounding strong with ringing cries
  Her names of joys and glories.
But when amid these cries of fame
She hears the earth one word proclaim,
With greatest joy she greets that name—
  Dolores.

For "Dolores" was her earthly share,
In grief and woe she deigned to bear
Christ's cruel Passion, Death and Care:
Yea, Sorrow was the weary stair
By which she reached her glories.
Mother of Sorrows, turn thine ear
To all thine own in sorrow here,
And hear the name to thee so dear—
Dolores.

For a Valentine

To Mary

Of yore you wrote upon my lips
White melodies;
And your finger-tips
Touched on my soul sweet ecstasies.
As when a bird 'mid flowers poses,
My heart was wreathed,
Like yours, with roses . . .
And even though, somehow unsheathed,
Their petals dropped, wilted and torn,
And like a bird
Among a thorn
My heart at first seemed left unheard—
I feel your heart, your lips, your fingers
Still play in mine
The tune that lingers
On this thorn-crowned valentine.

An Idyll Belvedere

Her fair foot rests upon the crescent moon,
Which lifts its prow from out a sea of clouds,

A silver boat that sinks not with her weight;
For hands ethereal seem to bear her form
Upon a mystic mist of lights celest,
Of rainbow sprays and shadows glorified.
Her folded hands speak thoughts reflected bright
Upon her stellar eyes that upward gaze
In joy triumphant over sorrow's mark
That once had been. The lavish hair
Repeats the rhythm of the envious clouds
Around her head. O lovely Maiden Face!
Delight of angel eyes, a maiden pure
In a gown of snow that falls upon the moon.
And from her hands, and 'neath her arm,
A folded mantle floats upon the mists,
An azure cloud that stole her richest blue
From out the deepest caverns of the skies—
Full many painters have exhausted Art
In bringing forth her beauty and her love.
How sweet her veiled form 'mid lilies poised!
How queenly and majestic with a crown
Of gold ir diadem of stars! And, too,
How pitiful and sorrowful and dear
Beneath her dying Son! But who of all
Can paint a lovely picture, fair to see,
To match the great Murillo's masterpiece,
"The Immaculate Conception?" Idyll pure—
Her fair foot resting on the crescent moon,
Which lifts its prow from out a sea of clouds;
Her tresses floating on a sea of mist;
Her eyes divine—O angels' sweet delight!
O Mary, chaste and loving, would I had
That artist's pure conception and his art,
To paint his masterpiece in glorious tones
Upon the lowly easel of my heart.

Thou Heardest First My Lullaby

Thou heardest first my lullaby,
Thy mother's happy, happy croon,
Before the angels sleeping nigh
Awoke and donned their silver shoon.

When every hill and valley rang
With all those tidings beautiful,
My song was over; yet I sang
Thee more, and still my heart was full.

The Heavens rejoiced, but after me,
The earth. And only God on high
First heard my voice; for 'twas not He
To whom I sang that lullaby?

O happy night for angel throngs,
When Heaven held no charms for them—
They sang that night their sweetest songs,
For Heaven then was Bethlehem.

But, Jesus mine, the world was still,
When first by me I saw Thee lie;
No angel chorus rose until
Thou heardest first my lullaby.

A Carol Mystic

You are the orient beauty, Love,
Of early morning,
And from your hues a mourning-dove
Her nest is dreaming of
Adorning.

She leans her head upon your breast
Of rainbow streamers,
And finds a warm and downy nest.
The dove and I are best
Of dreamers.

What makes your charming beauty, Love?
Could I but hear it
That Something tints your eyes above,
And lures to you a dove,
My spirit.

Would that the dove her nest could draw,
When you with mild eyes
Spread forth a bed of golden straw
And lay thereon with awe
The Sunrise.

To say I do not love the dawn
Could be no stranger
Than of my love for you were gone,
Had I been laid upon
The Manger.

Madonna by Murillo

"Here is no golden-crowned celestial queen
Such as Angélico could fitly paint."
—Charles Wharton Stork

What blithe archangel had this painter told
That man sees heaven best within his heart,
That he should to his sacred theme impart
An earthly motherhood, a human mold?
How lovingly does she her Babe enfold!

Such love needs no embellishment of art,
Portrayed so well in this earth's every part
Where mothers are and have a child to hold.
So might have been the mother that he knew,
Once when she held him in her arms benign;
A picture might this be of yours and you,
Perhaps, a portrait of myself and mine.
Madonna, making us perceive the true
Maternal Masterpiece of the Divine.

On a Street-car

(Christmas Eve)

Old lady, standing on the aisle,
And yet no sign of gloom,
Although the seats are filled awhile,
Because there is no room;

Smiling with your thoughts of joy,
Of someone on your lap,
You press your hand upon some toy,
The other on the strap.

Lady, I understand the plight
Of one sweet Lady whom
They turned away that Christmas Night
Because there was no room.

The Priestess

Mulier, amicta solis, et luna sub pedibus ejus.
—Apocalypse.

From the altar stone-steps of the moon
With You
And chasubled with the sun,

They come to me but soon depart,
As I will leave them,
All but You, You and the Priestess.

And ever it is she
Who comes, the queenly Priestess,
And I would have her pour within me
Your Sacrifice
Before I leave like those who leave me,
All but You, You and the Priestess
Who is ever with me,
From the altar stone-steps of the moon
Of Love
And chasubled with the Sun—
With You.

The Visitation

The first procession of Corpus Christi
Took place when Mary went in haste
Into the hill country.
Her journey nature graced
With a blue canopy
All about with white clouds laced;
Her path the wind with petals strew,
While birds sang hymns, and every tree
Its incense-scents of balsam blew.
It was the best Corpus Christi,
On this first Visitation Feast,
For she was monstrance as well as priest!

Doncella

(A Tempo di Spagna)

Girding the garden of God
And circling his cloud-lawned villa,

A wall stands, lofty and broad,
And on it the fair Doncella.
She leans from the wall so high
And calls me, the fair Doncella,
And fringes the glance of her eye
With the edge of a blue mantilla.

She laces the smile of her eye
With the hem of a blue mantilla!

Blue like the heavens, her shawl,
With lilies embroidered, presses
The snow-folds that 'round her fall
Ungirt, like her raven tresses,
Blue the mantilla that veils,
Unheeded, those raven tresses,
And blue is her look as it sails
On the billows of their caresses.

Sky-blue is her glance as it sails
On the billows of their caresses!
Oh, not that her fair request
The gatekeeper's heart would harden
Does she climb to the wall's high crest
That circles her Father's garden!
On wheat sheaves and vines she may
Climb up from her Father's garden,
Thus showing her lover the way
That leads past the gold-keyed warden.

She shows me the lovable way
That leads past the tear-stained warden!

I see her and hear her call,
She waves me the blue mantilla;

I must and will scale that wall
That girdles the cloud-lawned villa.
From grain field and grape-hung vine,
(My steps to the cloud-lawned villa)
On wheat sheaves and casks of wine,
I'll climb to the fair Doncella.

On wheat sheaves and casks of wine
I'll come to the fair Doncella;
I'll enter the garden of God
That lies in the cloud-lawned villa!

A la Conquistadora

Cuando DeVargas vino a dar
Auxilio a la ciudad,
[¿]Cuál fue el poder para vencer
I [Y] dar la libertad?
Tú Vencedora
Le fuiste, María,
Cuando la armada
Cantó de alegría,
"[¡]A la Conquistadora!"

Tu gran favor con bien amor
O nunca se olvidó.
Rogándote, tu Santa Fe
Por siglos lo guardó.
Pues Vencedora
Le eras, María;
Tu nombre siempre era
Canción de
alegría—
"[¡]A la Conquistadora!"

A La Conquistadora

When DeVargas came
To lend succor to the city
What strength did it take to win
and gain freedom?
You, Victorious One,
Were like the Virgin Mary to him,
When the armed forces
Sang with joy,
"Here's to the Conquistadora!"

Your splendid favor coupled with
kind love
Oh but he never once forgot
about it.
Beseeching you, your Santa Fe
For centuries he safeguarded.
Well Victorious One,
You are like the Virgin Mary
For your name was always
A song of joy to him—
"Here's to the Conquistadora!"

Celeste Virgen, ven, oir
    Con gusto mi canción.
Recibe hoy lo que te doy
    Con grato corazón.
        Tú Vencedora
No eres, María.
Por siempre y ahora
    Cantemos en día—
"[¡]A la Conquistadora!"

Celestial Virgin, come, listen
    With joy to my song.
Take today what I hereby give
    you
    With a thankful heart.
    You Victorious One,
Are our Virgin Mary,
For now and forever and now
    Let us sing a new day—
"Here's to the Conquistadora!"

Translated by Nasario García

The Virgin of Guadalupe

For a dress she wears the wild-rose,
For a cape the starry night,
And the sheen that frames her figure
Is the sun's resplendent light.

But her face is dark and slender—
"I am black but beautiful!"—
Not the gold-haired Queen of Heaven
With her features fair and full,

But the face of her who traveled
Down to Egypt's deserts dun,
Or who gently washed His garments
'Neath the Galilean sun.

Esther

My Lady Esther, beautiful
With beauty indescribable,
Of guileless grace and modest mien,

With much of handmaid and of queen,
Nor less of mother than of maid,
Dared stand in awe, yet unafraid
Of all the pains that death might bring,
Before the presence of her King.

Where no man dared approach, alone
She came and pleaded for her own,
Sure that her beauty would be heard
For me, whose life lay on his word.
Oh, never beamed a star so fair
As did my Lady Esther there,
For, Heaven's eyes be e'er so dear,
They lack the sparkle of a tear.

And that great King of mind unknown
By love was fixed fast to his throne,
Transformed by joy, to know that here
Was one whose love surpassed her fear.
Well might have Sheba's queen foregone
Not only all of Solomon,
But the whole world and everything,
For just a smile from such a King.

How much that smile did mean to me
My Lady Esther knows; for she
Of guileless grace and modest mien,
As much a handmaid as a queen,
Nor less a mother than a maid,
Dared stand alone and unafraid
Before her King, who smiled upon
Her tears, and said: "Behold, the Son!"

Hyacinth

Whence did the hyacinth grow,
So like a spindle spun with snow?
Did Mary, threading lambkins' wool
Around her distaff's giant spool,
Insert it in a flower-bed,
When Gabriel came to her and said:
"Hail Mary, full of grace art thou!"
And hence the flower we have now?

Mother's Day

In the Tenements

This is your feast-day, Madonna,
    I light you two candles to-day;
And it is my birthday, Madonna,
    Old Rosa is eighty this May.
But eighty is eighteen, Madonna,
    When you care for Rosa this way—
I'd hate to be an orphan, Madonna!

Christmas Lullaby

Sleep sweetly, Bambino, a lullaby low
Thy mother is singing so gently and slow,
While shepherds breathe softly the length of their flutes,
And angels play carols on viols and lutes.

Sleep lightly, Bambino, the lullaby swells,
And Mary's pure bosom with melody wells;
The flutes, lutes and viols now warble like birds,
And voices roll softly with heavenly words.

Sleep soundly, Bambino, the lullaby dies,
Thy Mother's own lashes lie nigh to thine eyes!
The flutes and the shepherds now lie on the straw,
And angels and viols grow silent with awe.

A Legend of the Holy Family—

They sat them down among the hollyhocks,
That rear their blossom crowns above the wall,
A mother and her boy. "These flowers tall,"
Quothe she, "Our people call St. Joseph's staffs.
These lilies, reaching for the bursting rose
Above them blowing, are the Virgin's hands."
They both in silence gazed from staff to rose,
From rose to lily, then the lovely three
They placed together. "Mother," said the boy,
"We have with us the Holy Family!"

She answered not, but gazed beyond the tiles
Of waving scarlet on the snowy walls
Upon a vastness of unchanging blue.
"She thinks of father," thought the boy, when, lo!
The lifeless azure lived, and far away
Dark specks appeared, and nearing, larger grew,
Until with joyous, merry twittering
They hovered, circling o'er the crimson roof,
And with their phantom shadow moistened it
A host of swallows! Fluttering together,
One by one, they perched upon its wavy crest,
Like soldiers side by side, or more like those
At church, in snowy robes and capes of black,
A chanting choir of Dominicans.

The boy picked up a broken tile, her hand
His fingers touched. "My son," she whispered low,

"Harm not the birds, the sweetest voice of God,
Much less these swallows, heaven's mellow lutes.
A lovely legend runs among our own
About our Lord and them. Long years ago,
When Herod ordered every infant slain,
The Holy Two left Bethlehem with Him,
The One Divine. When o'er the burning sands
They staggered, drowning in the desert heat,
Without a shade of palm or cloud, a flock
Of singing swallows suddenly appeared,
And, flitting close, they formed a canopy
Above the three."

And ere she spoke again,
The swallows flung themselves upon the air,
And soaring o'er the tiles, a flying matle,
Wet them with their shadows, then like smoke
Dissolved away, and left them dry again.

Cantares Franciscanos

Brown Shadow

I was looking from my window and my gazing fell upon
The brown shadow of a spire of an abbey on the lawn.
And I thought which was most worthy
    of a song upon the lyre—
The brown color of the shadow or the abbey or the spire.

Then I wondered why the shadow of
    the spire should be brown:
Was it just a cross' shadow, or
    St. Francis kneeling down?

There are landscapes etched with grace
    on every meadow, every lawn;
Yet, such scenes of depth and color
    from my fancy's care are gone.
Save—'Tis Heaven, sure, the vista that can readily surpass
The brown shadow of the spire of an abbey on the grass.

Stigmata of Saint Francis

My cross I took on me
As winds pick up a leaf,
Hoping to reach your Calvary
And be at least the thief.

The yoke is sweet and light,
The burden light and sweet,
But, oh! the time is gall and night
Before we both do meet.

Yet, must I follow still,
The while we seem to stop
Like two lone pines upon a hill

That never reach the top?
Dear Christ! at last I scan
La Verna's cliff-veiled side:
Complete the picture You began
And have me crucified.

Il Ricchio Poverello

St. Francis, it is writ of old,
Had money, also jewels bright;
A coin of silver, one of gold,
And diamonds animate with light.

He loved them so that he would sing
His sweetest canticles to them,
Saying that God had made no thing
So beautiful in coin or gem.

Thoughtfully wise and wisely sage,
Seeing himself about to die,
He left his sons a heritage
In the high vaults of the sky.

Through days and nights the ages run,
Through thefts of peace and spoils of wars:
His sons still have their golden sun,
Their silver moon and sparkling stars.

The Friar's Christmas Gift

With stainless hands the whirling snows
Have laid an ermine veil;
A starlight sheen from heaven glows
To brighten hill and dale.
Sweet-tongued chimes from cloister tower

Ring in the joyous morn;
Begins the Mass at midnight hour,
The eve when Christ was born.
A sickly novice keeps his cell,
Too weak his limbs to raise,
While in his soul the ringing bell
Stirs songs of love and praise.

"As these white snows divinely shine
Against this inky night,
So gleams thy Presence, Lord, near mine,
All radiant dazzling bright.
As these gray walls are guarding sure
The earth's unspotted gown,
So hast thou, Lord, my soul kept pure
Within this tunic brown.
My God, roll heaven's gates aside
And send Thy Son to earth—
Ah, close them not, but ope[n] them wide
For my immortal birth!"

The priest low o'er the altar bends,
The words their message give;
The gates roll back, and Christ descends
Again with men to live.
The gates close not, while angels fair,
Singing the Birth of Love,
With joy the friar's soul now bear
Beyond the gates above.
God in the novice, the novice in Him,
Sublime, eternal Feast—
Among the Saint and Seraphim,
The Offering and the Priest!

The Jester's Carol

Christ was born in a friary.
How long it must have been,
Since the inn was full and so lovingly
—An ancient Padre told me this—
The friars took them in.

Two friars lived in a convent wood
That stood near Bethlehem;
A friar grey in a greyish hood,
And cowled in brown, in chestnut brown,
The host that welcomed them.

They did their best and they gave their best
To them that Christmas night—
A bed of straw for their kingly guest,
Their breath to warm the little One
Against the winter's bite.

Yes, Christ was born in a friary,
How long it must have been,
Since the inn was full, and so lovingly
—An ancient Padre told me this—
The friars took them in!

Serus in Coelum Redeas

(Silver Jubilee, Fr. Urban)

A score and five pure lilies white
And ruddy roses sweetly twining
Adorn a silver altar bright
Of faithful toil and learning's light,
Of will and zeal to God resigning.

Like flowers fed by Heaven's dew,
May these, 'mid silvery sheen embracing,
Live on and blow with brighter hue,
For five and twenty years anew—
Of radiant gold an altar gracing.

Franciscan Poet

Be a poet like your Father,
Toiling not for earthly years;
Sing your lyrics in your sorrow,
Write your poems with your tears.

Then appear before the Master,
Fearing neither woe nor curse,
For the Book of Life will open
And reveal a Book of Verse.

Silly Lyric

Swallow, lovely swallow, called St. Francis to a swallow,
Leave the swallows that you follow
And recline within the hollow
Of my cowl, or follow still.

And the swallow saw the pillow from a
blowing blue-air billow.
Settled down upon that pillow,
Trilling lightly "Twillow—twillow—"
With her little yellow bill.

So they sang until the swallow fell asleep like any swallow,
While the saint, like any fellow,
Went and found himself a pillow
'Neath a willow on the hill.

In Memoriam

(Fr. Eligius Kunkel, O. F. M.)

May 30, 1927

The morning was leaden and ashen,
The trees were all blurred and blue,
The trees and the grasses were blue.
It was May, her last day, and her passing,
And the woodland was covered with dew
Which fell from the maples like teardrops
And melted the green into blue.

A friar stood watching in wonder
A statue he lovingly knew,
St. Anthony's figure in marble,
Like foam on the sad azure hue.
And the tears gently fell from the maples,
And some on his countenance blew,
Filling his eyes with their sadness
And flecking his cheeks with the dew.
Said the statue: "I weep for my brother,
Whom God took from men and from thee;
He is gone, brave and valiant helmsman
Of His ship on Life's turbulent sea.
He is gone, good and valiant helmsman,
To a harbor away from that sea,
To a harbor away from that sea.

"Souls out of the depths he saved many,
By his priestly immaculate hand,
By the strength of his anointed hand.
But, oh, my dear brother, the waters
How cruel they rose at his goal,
And snatched him while saving a body
That harbored a more precious soul.

"But why do I weep—is it envy?
Or envious sadness that he
Should be favored the death of a martyr,
A blessing not granted to me?
No, he dwells in the Heaven Franciscan
With Jesus and Francis and me,
And I weep that he left all in sorrow,
His brethren, his people and thee."
By the trills of the thrushes awakened,
The friar arose from the green,
For the grasses and maples were green.
Now the heavens were golden and azure,
And the woodland had found all her green;
And o'er him still gazed that white statue,
Smiling in Spring's sunlit sheen.

As if saying: "Arise, I have spoken,
Go, sing of my brother, the priest.
Sing loud of the hero and martyr,
Now happy in God's holy Feast.
Tell all of our brother, the Hero,
The Friar, the Martyr, the Priest,
The Padre Franciscan, the Priest."

To Saint Paschal

Paschal Baylon,
Paschal, the gentle,
Paschal, the shephered boy of Aragón!

Where drowsy torrents, waking on the rocks,
Lean from their dizzy beds against the sky,
And, combing on the crags their crystal locks,
Like fairies spread them on the grass to dry,
The shepherd keeps his flock upon the vale.

Beyond the rocks a distant warning peals,
Then, as the rising Phoebus shows the Grail,
The little Galahad in worship kneels.

The Vision calls: "Come to a sweeter meade—
Come, feed my sheep and with your little rod
The Lamb of Heaven keep—"
And down the valley where the torrents lead
The shepherd finds the pasturelanes of God!

A Seraphic Serenade

O'er the strings the minstrel's fingers
gently glide in tuneful songs,
As they seek the chord ecstatic that
will touch the theme he longs.

Soft awaken strains romantic, but
they sound too vague and bare,
Softer still his spirit brightens, and he whispers low a prayer.

Then in throbbing joy and gladness
does he touch the wanting chord;
Loud and grand it swells and echoes—joins
his voice in sweet accord.

'Tis not only love romantic that the bard will sing and play,
Love their is more swe[e]t and holy, where
all hearts may find a lay.

Not where pours the moon her radiance
on the rose-kissed balcony
Must the singer mold its silver to a golden melody.

But the soul must soar on upward, far beyond its silver hue,
To that throne of golden glory where the vision's ever new.

There romantic mellow melodies more may be made;
Glad the heart will sing with angels a seraphic serenade.

In the days when knighthood's flower
    blossomed forth in court and plain,
Lived a youth to knighthood given,
    heart and spirit, hand and brain.

Kind, in peace he loved his people,
    brave he fought in noble war;
Bright he shone to men and women,
    before God he beamed—a star.

For he sought no hand of mortal,
    nor the sword of gallant knight,
But the sweet Love-Grail of Jesus—
    long he wished that blessed sight.

God he loved and thus he wearied
    of the worldly and their ways;
In this Love he sought the silence
    far from men's disturbing gaze.

Thence, alone, he wandered regions
    of seclusion and of prayer,
Till he found a verdant country, verdant, ravishingly fair.

Vale of Prayer, of earth and heaven
    art the nearest, dearest tie,
Where the lover, love-enraptured, naught desires but to die.

Beautiful! here limpid streamlets
bubbled neither loud nor mute,
And the knightly poplars nodded to the breeze's silent lute.

Rich the mellow, fluting warbles of the skylark's piccolo,
Never ending, found their echoes in the cowled oaks below.

Ravishing, where gliding shadows,
bringing forth God's radiant Dove,
Hovered o'er the thorns of penance,
bearing roses of His Love.

Deep among the groves of silence,
where his truce with God he made,
Lone and sad, he found a maiden, like a jewel in the shade.

But how bright she beamed and sparkled
when she saw the light again,
How did shine her tears like diamonds
that she shed for erring men.

Clad in garments white he found her,
wreathed her brow with blossoms fair,
Like the graceful virgin lilac, wearing violets in her hair.

To his sylvan rose cathedral, up the lily-lined aisles,
Forth he led the radiant being to the One the world reviles.

Then he sang with angel voices his seraphic wedding-tide:
"God in Heaven, be my Father, Lady Poverty, my Bride!"

For this youth was holy Francis,
proud Assisi's dauntless knight,
Who had found, alone and weeping, Lady Poverty, his light.

Poverty! Pure exiled maiden, spurned
by man from whence she came,
Weeping for her own that hate her,
yet unwilling bear her name.

Thrilled his heart with sacred gladness,
gladness born of love divine,
Holy Francis vowed that ever would the exiled maiden shine.

To all men he showed the beauty,
wondrous beauty they had spurned;
But they saw no beauty in her,
called him fool, their backs they turned.

Won by meekness of the lover and
the chasteness of the bride,
Men again did call her mother, whom at first they did deride.

Straight the Poor Man of a Poor Bride
rose in sacred, deathless fame;
Men and nations through the ages
have since then revered his name.

"Sweet St. Francis," sighed the poet,
"would that he were here again!"
Sweet St. Francis still is living in the hearts of humble men.

Humble men! these are his children,
wearing robes of poverty;
Sweet St. Francis, he is humble, and
these humble men are he.

And the vale of Prayer is fertile, and her crystal waters sweet;
Art and Grace with Science burgeon
  at the great Creator's feet.

All these men dwell in that valley
  (that romance has seen no fall)
With their Father and his Lady and the God he called his all.

O how great the glorious Father!
  O how sweet and pure the Son!
O how bright the Holy Spirit!
  O how Francis loved them—One!

"God is One and God is Love,"
  how oft the bards these tidings call:
All true Love is loving Him because
  He's One and Love and All.

Francis loved in truth, "Our Father,"
  loved his brothers, beasts and men;
Loved the trees, the bees, the flowers,
  all beyond and in his ken.

All was song to him from heaven,
  sun and earth, the sea and air,
Sung to Jesus and his Mother in his holy Vale of Prayer.

Now the minstrel's fingers weary, and his voice is dying low.
Throbs his soul in joy ecstatic, joy that only Saints can know.

For his eyes have seen the Vision—soft
  the mystic colors fade—
Once again a string he touches—faintly dies his serenade.

Little Poor Man to Little Boy Blue

Lay aside the blue jeans, Little Boy Blue!
Far richer garments are waiting for you.
    Now, put on my brown,
    The hood and the gown,
And the girdle Big Brother of Padua knew—
Lay aside the blue jeans, Little Boy Blue.

Sheep on the meadow, lamb's in the thorn,
Far from the shepherd other ones roam.
Put on my habit, loud blow your horn,
Bring them together, lead them back home.

Harvest is golden, wheat and the vine,
Ready for reaping, but gleaners are few,
Master is waiting, waiting are mine,
Waiting for you, dear Little Boy Blue.

Lay aside the blue jeans, Little Boy Blue!
Far richer garments are waiting for you.
    Now, put on my brown,
    the hood and the gown,
And the girdle Big Brother of Padua knew—
Lay aside the blue jeans, Little Boy Blue!

The Fairy Friar

'Neath the whispering leaves of the greenwood,
I came on a fairy friar,
As he preached from a jack-in-the-pulpit
'Neath an arching of rose and briar.

His habit was cut from a brown leaf,
His girdle a spider made,

And the faithful that listened around him
Were the folk of the leaf and blade.

With a Paduan grandeur his sermon
Reechoed through columns of trees;
And his Chrysostom words were far sweeter
With the flowing pure gold of the bees.

How they feasted my soul with their sweetness,
Until I opened my eyes to pray—
Now the jack-in-the-pulpit was empty
And the sermon had faded away.

All the thoughts of the sermon have left me,
With their sweetness of heavenly lore;
Yet a key (they have told me) repeats them,
As it opens a Golden Door.

It may be that a priest at the pulpit
Might labor for words in vain—
And the thoughts of this elfin Franciscan
Will come to his mind again.

In Honorem

Joannis Duns Scoti

O Maria Immaculata,
Scoti tu victoria,
Sic concepta sicque nata
Es Minorum gloria.

Quando de Conceptione
Matris disputatio fit,
Summa Dei ratione
Ait Scotus: *Potuit.*

Dixit: Pater cum coelorum
Genitum monuerit
Homo fiat, templum purum
Praeparari *decuit*

Tandem Scotus cantem *jecit*
Congaudente Filio:
Deus Matrem *ergo fecit*
Sine labe in utero.

In Honor Of

Joannis Duns Scoti

Oh, Immaculate Mary,
You, the victory of Scotus,
So conceived and so born
Are the glory of the Minor
[orders].

When concerning the
Conception
Of the Mother there was a
debate,
With the highest reason of
God
Scotus said: *He could.*

He said: When the Father
deemed
That the Begotten of the
heavens
Should become a man, a pure
temple
Had to be made ready.

At length Scotus composed a
song,
While the Son rejoiced:
God *therefore made* the Mother
Without a stain in [her]
womb.

Translated by John M. Sharp

Jesum Liliaque

Ad. S. Antonium Patavinum:

Jesum liliaque gerens,
En miracula jam quaerens
    Te precatur populus;
Hunc, Antoni, semper cura
Invenique res, et jura
    Eis serva sedulus.

Nihil autem horum quaero,
Nil miraculorum vero,
    Sancte, facias in me;
Meme Jesulum dignare
Saltem paululum levare
    Meae cunis animae.

Jesus and Lilies

To St. Anthony of Padua

Bearing Jesus and lilies,
Lo, now seeking miracles,
The People beseech you;
Him, Anthony, always care
    for
And find the matters, and the
    oaths
Preserve for them sedulously.

However, I seek none of these
    things,
No miracles indeed,
Oh Holy One, may you
    perform in me;
May you deign for me;
To hold the Baby Jesus
At least for a brief moment
In the cradle of my soul.

Translated by John M. Sharp

Ventramour

Thus was the good youth Ventramour
Who would be Friar of Orders Grey:
To be content he must have more.

He would to pass the convent door
And live, meantime, the worldly way—
Thus was good youth Ventramour.

The best from out the friars' store
Was ever given him; but, nay,
To be content he must have more.

All drink he fancied from the shore
Of rivers on a rainy day.
Thus was the good youth Ventramour.

What came of him I know not, for
But this they know of him to-day:
To be content he must have more.

Now, whether thou be rich or poor,
Let never discontent thee sway;
Thus was the good youth Ventramour:
To be content he must have more.

Legend of The Bl. Ramón Lull, O.F.M.

Love was a wound, sweet in its painfulness,
To that Catalonian Cavalier,
Who, though first in war and last in fear,
Was vanquished by a woman's loveliness.
"Love is a wound: the breast I would caress
Hath wounded me and death is very near!"

He rode to her, at prayer in church, to hear
A happy answer to his warm address.
She turned to him and laid her bosom bare,
Her fair breast—with a cancer putrified.
He rode away and changed his sword for prayer . . .
"Love is a wound!" to all the world he cried.
"Painfully sweet, but undecayed,—and there
He dies for me, a red wound in His Side!"

Sonnet to a Modern Young Lady

To Clara bow, sprite woman of today,
Before her bend your free and unbowed head;
For she, not you, could find that coveted
And long-sought beauty-love for which you pray.
She, she was charming, young, like you, and gay,
With woman's poise and independent tread;
But she heard love, when called, and never fled—
And when Love came she did not turn away.
You did not flee, O Clara saint, you came,
When Jesus gently called you to His side.
You blushed, indeed, but not with fear or shame—
For Beauty's gate had suddenly stood wide,
And to the portals of Love's lasting fame
The loving Bridegroom led a willing Bride!

Father and Son Before Saint Anthony

Now, gaze, dear child, into Saint Anthony's face,
And mark its tender love with ecstasy.
He holds a Baby—so—like you and me,
But, oh, how different the poise, the grace.
Now look into your father's eyes and trace
A tender love, but also misery;
For ever in that Paduan's face I see

A joy that makes my soul an empty place.
You are the sweetest gift, the richest boon,
That any mortal can from God demand.
Yet, though I love you as the beaming moon
That lights the darkness with His fire-brand—
My choice was poor: to hold you here and croon,
I would not hold my God upon my hand!

Franciscans in China

I tried to picture you in no uncertain lines
Upon a delicate screen of Orient art
Where flat-topped, antler-bowed black pines,
With blue-mist mountains in their wake,
Step to the water's edge, much like a hart . . .
And you were the crystal lake
That lent them all a living counterpart.

I tried to see you as the saffron moon
That no Great Wall could ever
Keep from entering to gild the rice;
Or like the lotus, floating at midnoon,
A flash of white upon the yellow river.
And you even appeared, zestful as spice,
To be the breath of sun and wind so free,
Driving the stench and gloom from narrow aisles,
And giving motion, hue, and certainty
To the roofs of Cathay, waving gracefully
In tiers of blue and green and yellow tiles
From the mountain to the sea.

But, last night at Benediction, when
The smell of incense brings a caravan
Of thoughts out of the East,
I saw you, each a grain of incense, fly

In spotless smoke before the priest—
And the prayer of China stormed the sky.

If Miracles

"If miracles thou fain wouldst see:
Lo! Error, death, calamity,
    The leprous stain, the demon flies,
    From beds of pain the sick arise!"
Thus sing the friends of Anthony.

The unbeliever swears that he
Finds nothing but vain mummery
    In what he holds before his eyes—
        "If" miracles.

Yet, more approach on bended knee
To bring God's favored son their plea;
    And to the skeptic's deep surprise,
    Rechanted louder through the skies,
Resounds the Saint's Responsory—
        "If miracles . . ."

Antonian Thoughts

"Mid the greenwood beeches, by the waving ferns,
Hid among their mossy roots and elfin glades
That shade the butterflies, they came, the two, and sat."

Daddy turned his paper news aside and peeped—
Gladly drinking in their Grandma's baby words
He spied his little boy and girl. The tale went on:
"Tree and flower stretched to see the two. One sat
(So like an angel) 'mid the daisies 'neath the roof,
Low, dewy, sparkling leaves; He nestled close,

Oh, close against his breast, and dear St. Anthony
A-thrilled with joy was then. Enrapt with love he kissed
The fragrant locks upon the Baby's head, and spoke
Endearing words, and sang Him lullabies which Mother,
Tender Mary, crooned within their little door.
For Anthony was Joseph's neighbor near that door.

"How his heart throbbed out with joy and love,
Now that Mary trusted him with Jesus babe
Beneath the greenwood leaves. And here among the ferns
He picked for Him the vestment colors of the Mass.
Violets, trembling with the weight of fairy dew,
Briar roses, bleeding from the darts of bees,
Twinkling aspen greens and snowy lily cups,
Winking fern-seed eyes of black below the singing
Grass—Now Jesus had the vestment colors for His Mass."

Daddy set his paper down and stared at them.
Wild thoughts—"Ignorance"—arose; but then,
Gladly smiled the father, smiled on Innocence,
Mild Innocence. And Anthony in Heaven
Smiled . . .

Hymn of the Brown Marines

From a fortress of Assisi, seven hundred years agone,
Went a battle-cry that never died and still is echoed on;
Over palm and pine and cactus hear the message that it tells:
"Preach the gospel to the Saracens and the other infidels!"

Chorus:
  Onward, soldier-lines of brown,
  Like your forebears of renown,
  Tighten up your woolen cords around
    your uniforms of brown.

On, Marines of God in brown,
On through wilderness and town,
To the outposts of the sunrise, to
    the shores where it goes down!

First to land upon the New World,
    first in China and Japan,
Guards of Palestine and Barbary,
    to far-off Hindustan;
Old Damascus and Quivira, these are
    fields of bloody scenes,

Red are Peking, Nagasaki, with the
    blood of God's Marines!

When the nations and the peoples out
    of every pole and zone,
Have been gathered for the reckoning
    before God's judgment throne,
They will see St. Francis standing
    and they'll wonder more and more
Where they saw that Brown Crusader
    and his uniform before!

Vision of Fray del Alba—

Ah, thrice happy youth, if in blossoming years,
In thy long days of bliss without worry or fears,
To thy heart speaks a Voice from the one Royal Throne,
That sweet Voice of the King who would make thee his own;
When the world spreads its charms to entice thee away,
Ah, remember his promise—"No man I betray!"
Mayst thou learn from this tale of a rescued vocation,
To rely on His word when assailed by temptation.

'Twas the time of midsummer, a dark, gloomy night,
That I lay almost vanquished and worn in the fight
With the foes of my soul, who in gruesomest form,
Waged a war in my conscience, a most furious storm.
Yea, the lure of the world in my sight deigned to revel,
And my heart suffered much from the flesh and the devil.
So that wearied, exhausted, and crazed by this din,
I would spurn my vocation and trade it for sin.

The wan moon o'er the ink of the sky slowly slid,
And the stars seemed to mock from the firmament's lid.
The dry air, hot and stifling, my stiff being covered,
O'er my spirit the phantoms of gloom grimly hovered.
I was clutched by the claws of the sleep of despair,
And I burned, it seemed ages, in fear's scorching flare.
Torn my body by talons, and flogged with wings,
I was tormented and wounded by dank, oozy things.

All these black, slimy demons with hideous alarms
Dragged me out to the sea with their slimier arms.
Amid gnashing and wailing and cries in the dark,
I was flung on a creaking and black hellish bark.
On this grim derelict I did plow out to sea,
While I writhed on the deck in a deep agony.
Lo! a mountain of brine o'er the vessel did loom,
And she woefully perished with loud shrieks of doom!

I was tossed on the waters and lashed by the brine,
All alone, without hope, and of help not a sign.
The dark skies and the clouds split with flashes of light,
And they threatened with volumes of lightning bright.
Through the waves for a long, cruel spell I had swum,
Now my soul and my body were wearied and numb.

Yea, my conscience was lost in a fastness of gloom,
And, despairing, I longed for the ocean's vast tomb.

But, alas, sinful me! how despairing raved I,
Not to pray for that succor that dwelleth on high.
Still, from God came the aid, for a vessel drew near;
'Twas named "Hope" and was manned by a saint-visaged seer.
His brown robe and white cord were familiar to me;
I had seen that sweet aspect, yet who could he be?
Twas St. Francis Seraphic of sweet memory!
Had God sent him to save me and calm this mad sea?

With his kind tender arms the good Saint made me free
From the clutch of the raving and turbulent sea.
Oh, how soothing to me was his sweet holy presence,
Which instilled in my being His Love's purest essence.
As we sailed to a shore o'er the calm rolling waves,
In my heart grew a peace with the kind God who saves;
My unseen guardian Angel I gratefully praised,
To the Mother of sinners my soul I then raised.

Then we stepped on a shore that was rugged and steep,
And stood near a mountain that rose from the deep.
Like a lance it shot upward and pierced a thick cloud,
And its summit a veil of pure mist did enshroud.
A long path steeply wound up its steep craggy side,
That on top of the summit the cloud, too, did hide.
But still far, far beyond where these vapors did rise,
Gleamed a beckoning haven of God's Paradise.

As up the steep pathway we joyfully walked,
The Poor Man of Assisi of saintly things talked.
He spoke of the darkness that held heathen nations,
Of the need of more heralds, of priestly vocations.

Soon we reached the high summit—a Paradise rare;
It was mantled with verdure and flowers all fair.
Every petal and leaf beamed with gladness of day,
While the air bore the fragrance of blossoming May.

And now far, far below, the long roadway still wound,
O'er it masses of men came in deep sorrow bound.
As they climb up the mountain, all gray like the sod,
The saint showed me the ones that were chosen by God,
But who spurned their vocations and followed the world,
And, alas! all too late, had the truth been unfurled!
For despising the calling which once had been offered,
For follies committed, they terribly suffered.

To the top of the mountain these poor men trudged on—
Of a sudden the clouds from the summit were gone!
Then a blinding pure radiance of brightness untold
Softly blended in colors of silver and gold.
On a white gilded dais, all radiant and bright,
Shone the Queen all majestic, the lily all white;
Sat the Maiden, the Mother, all lovely and sweet,
'Twas Immaculate Mary, with Saints at her feet.

Good Francis then signed to his own sons in brown,
Who on earth bore the Cross and in turn wear the Crown.
All the friars who heeded and followed his Call,
Who took up the great motto: "My God and my All!"
The three Orders of Francis all kneeling beneath,
Around the White Throne wove a beautiful wreath.
Saintly priests, holy brothers, and virgins knelt there,
All the fruits of his garden, his flowers most fair.

At the sight of this vision entrancingly fair,
The great wish of my heart I poured forth in a prayer.

"Oh, where is my God and the pure Seraphim,
All those sweet, smiling Cherubs who sing around Him?
Tell me, where is the Christ of our poor fallen race?
Oh, do show me that kingly and radiant Face.
Show me God in His glory and heavenly splendor,
Show me Him and His Love and that Heart sweet and
    tender!"

"Tis the faithful departed alone see His Face,
And a few living mortals who walk in His grace.
You are still of the earth," made answer the Saint,
"And the glory you saw was but meager and faint.
When the roses of dawn angels pin on the sky,
And the sheen of the morning is purpling and nigh;
When the silver and gold of my Brother the Sun
Into oceans of azure sky glistening run,

"To the chapel make Haste at the Angelus call;
'Round the altar the glories of Heaven will fall.
The red tears of the grape in the chalice's hand
Will be red Precious Blood shed in Abraham's land.
The white hearts of the wheat, the God-chosen grain,
Will become our Lord's Body on Calvary slain.
In the priest's sacred hands your eyes shall behold
True God and True Man as the Master foretold!"

From afar came sweet strains, like the heralds of day—
Lo! The Saint and the vision both faded away.
While the music of Seraphim reechoed and soared,
In ravishing melody sang praise to the Lord:
"All praises to Thee, our God from above!
    Holy, Holy, Father of Might!
All worship be Thine, O sweet Son of Love!
    Holy, Holy, Spirit of Light!

Holy, Holy, Lord God, our voices ascending
Shall praise and adore Thee with glory unending!"

When the great gory giant had wounded the clouds,
And had thrust his fierce gaze through the vanishing shrouds;
As the gleam of his eyes 'gan to play on my bed,
I awoke from my slumber of bliss and of dread.
The night's joys and its horrors, how true they did seem;
Then I knew the true worth of this soul-piercing dream.
I had sinned and had neared the abyss of my fall;
I resolved in my heart to follow God's call.

The shrill note of the quail from her home in the lea,
And the coo of the mourning-dove's sweet reverie;
All the music enchanting from flutes of the birds,
Sweetly bore to my memory the saint's parting words.
Like seraphic pure voices in soft harmony,
Came the peal of the Angelus' sweet melody.
With my heart filled with gladness and purest delight,
To the chapel I hastened to witness the Light.

From the sun streamed a glory, a heavenly splendor,
Through the windows beamed colors enchantingly tender.
In a hushed sacred silence the Mass had begun,
Rose the priest's holy words in the Name of God's son.
And the soft soothing sound of the silvery bell,
Made the priest's holy words in divine rhythm swell.
Yet, more glorious and shining, more pure than the dawn,
I beheld my dear Lord, the Omnipotent One.

As if softly my spirit by seraphim tended,
A peace 'round me hovered when Mass had been ended,
A divine grace from heaven which earth cannot give,
And which teaches poor sinner for Savior to live.

Like the touch of the breeze on the harp of a rill,
Like the song of the leaves, neither rustling nor still,
Like the singing of grasses and flowers that nod
To the breeze—from my heart rose a hymn praising God!

"O my God, in the Being and Works I rejoice.
Evermore shall I hear Thy heartening Voice.
Lord, grant me the gift, the joy and the crown,
Always to serve Thee, a friar in brown.
Loving Thy Praises and praising Thy Love,
My gaze shall be fixed on the things from above;
May I follow, unchanging, Thy heavenly call,
Anew pledge my being, my will, and my All."

Vignettes

From the Life of St. Anthony

I
Son of Bouillon

Lady Teresa, good and queenly wife
Of one of Lisbon's peers, Martin Bouillon,
Still lingered at the great cathedral door,
Her little son beside her. From within
Still came the deep and measured sacred chant
Of ermined canons in the chancel choir.

"Sweet Mother," said the boy, "you say the priest
Was holding the Child Jesus during Mass—
Might I not do likewise when I am grown?"
The Lady, turning to the purpled canons,
Looked with that look of hopeful joy
That pious mothers have, whenever priests
Attend at bright and solemn liturgies.

"Ay, my Fernando, be it so," she said.

A baker's boy passed by, crying his wares,
Long loaves of bread, and young Fernando spoke:
"Dear Mother, I do love the sight of bread;
But, when I grow, I want none else than that
Which people neither buy nor sell." And she,
Catching a Latin hymn-phrase from the choir,
So like unto their native Portuguese,
Breathed to herself: "Behold the Bread of Angels!"
Then playfully: "You talk so strangely, son,
As though you read some ancient sacred book.
I should have named you after my great Saint,
Saint Anthony of Egypt!"

Said the boy:
"Sweet Mother, you might call me that, perhaps,
When I am grown and hold with my own hands
The Infant Jesus, like the priest at Mass."
"Ay, son," she sighed. "God's Will be done!"

II
The Son of St. Augustine

The silence of Coimbra's royal church
Was broken by the fervent matin tones
Of white-robed forms along the choir stalls;
And, as the verses flowed, one voice rose high
Above the rest, like an archangel's call
Amid a choir of angels; thus they sang,
These Canons Regular of St. Augustine.

Young Don Fernando, he whose voice rose high,
Whose noble kin would fain have made him be
A purpled canon or a cardinal,

Came forth to chant a lection of the day.
With "The Words of Saint Augustine, Bishop,"
He intoned the sermon on the martyrs.
And his voice began to tremble now
To the quiver of his white-draped frame,
For, laid in state before the chancel rail,
Were five Franciscan friars who had won
The martyr's palm among the Saracens.

What strange emotions gripped Fernando's soul,
Just as he sang the wise Augustine's words:
"And who is he who well can follow in
The footsteps of the martyrs? I reply:
"Not only them, but also Christ Himself,
If we desire, can we imitate!"
This was his sign, he knew, and this his call,
Thrice-sanctioned by the Doctor-Saint himself;
And, straightway, Don Fernando had resolved
To follow and to imitate.

And so,
The angel of light put off his robes
Of flowing white, and took a friar's garb
That made him shine a seraph of love;
The canons wept, when Frei Antonio left,
But their Abbot said: "God's Will be done!"

III
The Son of St. Francis

The verdant Umbrian valley waved with brown,
As countless friars sat upon the grass,
For quaint Assisi could not well contain
This great Franciscan Chapter. In their midst

Brother Elias talked; close at his feet
A little man was seated silently,
And on each hand and foot he bore a wound,
And in each bleeding wound there was a nail.

Unknown to all was Friar Anthony.
The hand of sickness had just snatched away
His martyr's crown upon Algerian sands.
And fateful storms, away from Spanish shores,
Had blown him to an alien coast.—But, oh!
What consolations soothed his tired soul
When he beheld that little man with wounds
Upon his hands and feet! He melted at
His Father Francis' meekness and reserve;
For, even though he wore upon his limbs
The scarlet seals of Christ, stamped by His Hand,
Said scarce a word. Then Anthony recalled
And better understood that fervent cry
Of Paul: "But God forbid that I should glory,
Save in the Cross of our Lord Jesus Christ;
By whom the world is crucified to me,
And I to the world!"

Now, when the brethren
Turned their footsteps home, the homeless one
Had none to seek, until he was assigned
Unto the lone and darksome hermitage
Of Monte Paolo. No superior knew
This youthful priest to be above them all
In learning, parentage, and piety.
A prouder spirit would have frowned, but he,
Still mindful of the little Wound-marked Man,
Hummed to his hear: "God's holy Will be done!"

IV
The Son of the Testament

The new priests rose, the oil of joy yet fresh;
The bishop, mitred still, turned to the ranks
Of Friars Preacher and of Minor Friars
That lined the chancel of Forli's cathedral.

He bade an old Franciscan father preach,
But Monte Paolo's aged guardian said:
"My age and weakness, Lordship, you do know,
And how dare I to preach, when in our midst
We have the preaching Sons of Dominic!"
The white Dominicans were unprepared
And with alarm declined; while even those
Famed orators among the Minors paled,
And each one humbly passed the honor on
To his unwilling neighbor. Then a thought
Came to the troubled guardian, and he spoke
In whispered accents to his young companion.

Obeying, Anthony arose and bowed in prayer.
The bishop scanned a book; the friars smiled.
But, scarcely had his first faint words begun,
When gospel text was laid aside, and, lo!
Each could have sworn he heard an angel's voice,
Telling the Scriptures and the Church's lore
In some celestial wise before undreamt.
Such love, such eloquence, it seemed his tongue
Had touched a honeycomb of Nazareth,
Or kissed the bleeding lips at Calvary!—
And all bowed 'neth the seraph-flame of Francis
That blazed upon the torch of Dominic,
And whispered: "Never spake man like this man."

"Why has such light, such light," the bishop asked,
Over his open gospel, "stood so long
Under a bushel?" But the guardian said:
"Such things the Lord alone can hide, and they
Await, not on our efforts, but His Will!"

V
The Son of the Eucharist

Within the chapel dark a red light trembled
As in awe, and on the altar step
A friar knelt; but, when the rainbow hues
Of bright-stained windows fingered on his cowl,
He rose, vested for Mass, and day began.

The multitudes on Bourges' streets made way,
As, Anthony, surpliced and stoled, came forth,
Bearing his King beneath a ritual veil.
Small wingless angels paved his path ahead
In fresh mosaics laid with petals,
Till they reached the city square, and there
A group of men were waiting with a mule.
A circle, guarded with a million eyes,
Enclosed the men, the beast, and Anthony;
And, when the choicest grains were placed before
The half-starved animal, it turned away
Toward the friar's breast, as though to ask:
"Is that not, He whom once an ass did bear
Into the city gates, and people threw
Not flowers, but the palms of victory?
Is that not he for whom an ass declined
To feed, so that its nostrils and its mouth
Be free to warm His naked little Self
Upon the straw-filled manger?" In this wise,

It knelt down, graceful in its clumsiness,
And would not rise until the friar's word
Had bidden it to rise and eat, amid
A silence worth a thousand cheers.

That eve,
Beneath the trembling light the friar knelt
In humble awe. "Sweet Sacrament," cried he,
"I thank thee for the wonder Thou hast wrought
Through me this day; but grant that painful praise,
This chalice of renown, may pass me by—
Yet, not my will, but Thine!" And day was done.

VI

The Son of Nature

A river weds the sea near Rimini,
And where her veil of crystal flows upon
The blue robe of the brace Adriatic, stood
A friar, raising both his arms aloft.
Beside him on the shore, a multitude
Of many-colored groups kept surging close
From out the walls of nearby Rimini.

Now Anthony was preaching, not to men,
But to a large concourse of eager fish;
For men had mocked and driven him away
From Rimini. But Anthony had said:
"The[e], if you care not for the word of God,
The fish, as it is written, Him shall bless."
When he began to speak the waters moved.
Lithe silver shapes leaped from the crystal river,
As though to catch his words; and from the sea
A horde of watery monsters showed their heads

In solemn earnestness while men looked on.
As Francis once had preached to all the birds,
And often drew the woodland creatures near,
To hear him speak of God, so Anthony
Preached to the fish. Perhaps, someone has said,
They took him for that Saint; but others say
The fishes knew he was the Son of Francis!
And so it came to pass that all these folk,
Both young and old, began to beat their breasts
And loud bewail their gross impiety.
For God had justly put their pride to shame
Through this great miracle.

Said Anthony:
"In the name of the forgiving Father,
I all forgive, and bid you bless the Hand
That for His purpose works such deeds.
His Will be done!"—Thereon they praised God where
The river weds the sea near Rimini.

The Barefoot Boy

The barefoot boy is gone from home,
But will come back anon;
And though he sing of silver shoon,
He'll come with sandals on.

Cantares Varios

Canticle of the Rainbow

Blue is the Warble of the Flute

Wake me the morning and wake me the birds,
And freshen their throats with the heaven dew,
Lure me their melodies, warble their words,
And then, Brother Man, I will think of you.
I shall hear your voice and the soul of you,
When they sing—
And I'll sing with the birds
And I'll sing
With you.

Green is the Whisper of the Harp

We love the refrain and the chorus
That answer the song of day,
And the noise of the grass that is growing
In the pools of the dew of May,
In the pools of dew.
Brother, sing the refrain and the chorus,
For your joy makes the song of day,
And I'll sing and rejoice in the May
With you.

Purple is the Sound of the Cello

When my thoughts sink deep about me,
And my singing is profound,
I sing alone;
When I am sad you sing without me,
And I alone
Must hear their deep and solemn sound.

I would not have around me
Your heart its song intone,
If it weighed my soul and bound me
Like my own.

Red is the Blast of the Trumpet

Now the long carefree note of the song
Resounds with a tremulous peal,
And I fling me away on the wing
Of the melody zephyrs I feel.
And you, Brother, fall with the darts
That are flung from the bow of song,
For the heart is free, the spirit is free
There is song in the hearts
Of you and me.

Golden is the Murmur of the Violin

Dreaming the songs of dreamers
I sing of you
In song and dream.
Singing the dreams of singers
I dream of you,
And dream is song, and song is dream . . .
Thus it is when the night has come,
And, though I am alone,
The song I sing within my dream
Is you.

A Rainbow is the Voice of the Organ

Thanks to the Creator for the wonderful day,
For the morn and the noon

And the sun and the dew and the birds and you.
Thanks be to Him for the eve and the night,
For the dusk and the moon
And the sleep and the dreams and you.
Thanks for the song of the universe,
For the joys, for the thoughts profound,
For the merry verse and the solemn sound
That freely are sung and freely abound
In me and you.

Jesus at the Well

Give me to drink this desert wine,
This water welled by men.
Amen, I say, but drink of mine . . .
You shall not thirst again.

Give me to drink, for I am I,
Begging from earthly jars,
Who plunged the Dipper in the sky
And splashed the night with stars!

To Witter Bynner

"And it is you this time that are the beloved stranger . . .
Approaching ever on a winged horse, like yours,
And bringing me a living star—"

An eager nestling chirped and wished to sing
The songs imprisoned in its memory;
One gentle note of courage served to bring
A pleasing, though imperfect melody.

One little note, Beloved Stranger—thine!
Unlocked a courage from its silent thrall:

"I like your poetry (O kindly line!)
But, really, I don't like you at all!"

A New Year Lyric

With palsied step his way pursuing
Plods on a feeble man and old.
And softly on our doorstep cold
He lays a bundle faintly cooing.
It is a babe the North Wind wooing,
Telling the breezes keen and wild
That he himself ere long a child
Must bear, through snow his way pursuing.

New Year! Fair Babe of wondrous blessing,
Thou innocent, naked, smiling tot.
Oh, may we dress thee as we ought,
With softest silks thy softness pressing,
With purest veils thy form caressing—
And then, ah, then, when thou art old,
Again wilt bring for us to hold
Another child of wondrous blessing.

Christmas in Heaven

They tell me, angels, that you flail
A wheat that on the clouds doth grow,
And blow to earth the chaff so frail,
That fleecy whiteness we call snow.
Oh, tell me, angels, is it so?

They say you make an angel bread
Which, blest by priestly hands you know,
On Christmas Night to you is fed,
When Christ again is born below.
Oh, tell me, angels, is it so?

And yet, they say you envy me,
Who feels the kiss of Christmas snow,
While in my heart none else than He
Has made His dwelling here below.
They tell me, angels, this is so!

Little Christmas

A Child's Tale

Three cherubs slept all night till morn,
The night when Jesus Christ was born.

And when they woke they cried in vain,
Because they wished Him born again.

The talk of Heaven was the birth
Of Jesus, Son of God, on earth.

The angel hosts sang loud and glad,
But these poor cherubim were sad.

They cried like poor forgotten boys
Who got no pretty Christmas toys.

And just because they slept all night
They missed the first sweet Christmas sight.

The Angel Gabriel came to them
And told the tale of Bethlehem.

Brave Michael offered them his spear
But neither cherub tried to hear.

But more they wept, till Raphael thought
Of one sure cure he had forgot.

He drew a cloud aside, and by
Them was a window in the sky.

With eager eyes the cherubs three
Leaned out of Heaven's halls to see.

And far below upon the earth
They saw the Lord's poor place of birth.

But where was Michael? Long they gazed—
when high he soared with shield that blazed.

His golden shield shone like a star!
Where did he throw its rays so far?

Oh, down he turned the light to earth,
Upon the Savior's place of birth.

And o'er a distant desert waste
They saw three camels trod in haste.

Each camel bore a man from far,
Who gazed with joy at Michael's star.

They reached a stable where the rays
Had guided them for many days.

They were three wise and holy kings
Who brought the King their richest things.

Now, these three cherubs gladly smiled,
Like weeping babies reconciled.

One cherub asked, "Oh, is this then
The Night of Christmas done again?"

And Gabriel answered: "Not at all
'Tis Little Christmas for angels small!"

Ruth

What prompts you to stop at your work in the grainfield
And poise in your wondering grace for an instant,
Like a lark from her nest in the wheat newly startled
By the fall of a footstep, approaching, though distant?

Do the sheaves that you hold in the arms of your beauty
Surprise you with thoughts that are silently said
By your tresses, like straw to be tossed in a Manger,
And your whiteness, like grain to be made into Bread?

The Holy Innocents

They could not wait for Christ to die
And rise in glory from the earth;
These little Stephens, lily-high,
Bore bloody witness to His Birth.

Like rosebuds from the bushes torn,
Men plucked them from their mother's breast,
Leaving a sharp and crimson thorn
Where every silken bud had pressed.

They rolled like grapes strewn by the wind,
Their virgin wine staining the sands,
Before their angel guides could find
Palm-leaves to fit their little hands.

O ruddy grapes! O roses red!
O martyred dolls with upturned eyes!
A perfume is the blood you shed—
The first-pressed wine for Paradise!

Simon Peter

A thundering cloud the sun denied
When 'neath the midnight stars he crept;
At dawn he met His glance—and sighed,
Then turned his face to earth—and wept.

Saint Therese

All praise the greatest Scientist
By whom all beauty grows,
Who from a little fleur-de-lis
Could make a little Rose.

First Poem

Today fresh flowers the altar adorn,
And sweeten the breezes that blow;
Tomorrow they'll lie, things faded and torn,
No tear for their passing will flow.

So, too, in the morn of this early life,
Youth's graces and charms are displayed;
Soon evening falls, makes an end of the strife—
'Neath the earth each glory is laid.

Mother

Thou art the song of God's love,
A golden gift divine.
A temple white for me, love,
A grotto and a shrine,
Where breathes thy heart His fragrant love,
And blows it into mine.

Through thee I see my God's love,
    Who fashioned from the sod,
From earth of Mother Eve, love,
    The Mother pure of God,
The Lily chaste, the whitest One
    That bloomed from Jesse's rod.

Praised be the Lord's divine love
    For making love like thine;
Live ever Mary's sweet love
    And e'er be thine and mine,
That long I may His fragrance breathe
At thy maternal shrine.

Seminarian's Prayer

Dear Lord, I heard Thy loving Call,
    "Come follow Me."
I left my home, my loved ones, all,
    To follow Thee.
My parents dear I left behind
    And followed Thee.
Lord, give them life that they may find
    A priest in me.
And when they both for Heaven yearn,
    Take them to Thee,
That there they wait for my return
    To live with Thee.

The Little Flower

A rare little flower grew far, far away,
A rose in a beautiful garden.
It drew all its life from a heavenly ray
And towered all fair over fleur-de-lis gay,

All pure in that far away garden.

It bloomed and lived on 'til the cold, biting fall,
Most bright in the beautiful garden.
The Master all-wisely plucked flower and all,
To bloom in a holier garden.

Brighter and redder, more lovely it grew
Each day in that beautiful garden.
Like incense its fragrance, how sweetly it blew,
And o'er all the cloisters a gladness it threw
That spread even far from the garden.

The Master was pleased with the pure holy flower,
The rose in the lone convent garden.
He lifted it up to His own sacred Bower:
Since then fall the petals in one rosy shower
From the Rose in His Paradise Garden.

Prayers

They stand and wait in countless rings,
With folded hands and folded wings,
A holy Throng of heavenly Things.

And when we pray, how sweet they nod;
They soar afar, the clouds they trod,
And bring our love and praise to God.

Even Song

Little Katy did, sing to me
Those vespers that move the soul,
With the scarlet sun drinking day
At the brim of the golden bowl.

When in the evening still
I hear the insects whirring,
Their accents loud and shrill
Seem truly sweet and stirring.
I think how oft our song,
Our vespers sent to heaven,
Must sound to God ere long
Like insect chirps at even.

Little Katy did sing to me
Those vespers that move the soul,
With the setting sun drinking day
At the brim of the golden bowl.

Chancel Light

To thee admiring hearts all speak in praise,
Wild flower of the latest man-made light,
Fair hand that parts the curtains of the night
Before the dawn begans those golds to raise.
Thy mellow flame is not to blind or daze;
The ancient gods loomed dim above thy sight;
To shine and worship was thy sacred right
Where Solomon in glory could not gaze.

And now, Chancel Lamp, no light has yet
Enjoyed the blessed favor granted thee.
The sun is born in glory, but to set,
While thou dost watch and guard incessantly
The Self-same One who watched at Olivet—
Oh, would I had thy burning constancy!

At Night

At night the lovers find their sweetest dreams,
While haunting music, sounding sweeter then,

Finds pleasure in their burning hearts. And men
Who toil and sweat beneath the sun, it seems,
Seek peace and comfort in the dark. Moonbeams
Open wide the owl's books, and when
They fade, the lurking thief is out again.
And all the world that's left, that daytime stream
Of people, is asleep. But thou, dark night,
Thou art to some the time of thought and prayer,
When heaven closer steals to earth, and light
More charming than the moon's reposes there.
At night, true love and peace the heart delight,
And God and Heaven whisper everywhere.

I Sat with Sorrow

I sat with sorrow 'neath a blowing tree,
And watched a fountain endless sprays unfurl,
Full jewelled streamers twined with braids of pearl
That danced a wink upon a silver sea
And blew in rainbow mists on him and me.
The leaves above turned greener with each spray,
And I perceived a Truth but could not say
A word—then sorrow spoke the simile:
"O Cross, thou art the fountain never dry,
Thy sweet, sweet wood an altar, for 'twas laved
With Blood of Him who deigned on thee to die;
'Til to this day from that last dying sigh
God's faithful by thy cooling stream are saved
From thirsting Hell to Heaven's Feast on high."

Books

Your honeyed lips are like the aspen leaves
That drink the spray beside a forest stream,
Forever whispering things that make me dream
Of fragrant sylvan shades, of golden sheaves.
On them I feel the mighty sea that heaves
In restless sleep; their bubbling nectars seem
To raise me high to fair Creation's beam,
Where I can lean—and peep 'neath Heaven's eaves
And hear and see the sweetest things. Yes, books,
You're each a friend, and every page a part
Of all that is; and anyone who looks
For progress, travel, inspiration, art,
Needs but to seek your sacred flowered nooks,
And from your lips' sweet treasure fill his heart.

Sonnet

On Reading Macbeth

The deed is done, and crowned king Macbeth,
For Duncan's murdered by his sleeping groom.
Rejoicing for the haughty Queen, to whom
Success he owes. But murder's stain beneath
The bloody palm remains. Like fetid breath
The ghost of Banquo haunts the banquet room;
The Lady's sleeping lips wake words of doom,
And, last, the wages of their sin is death,
For death must follow death. The neighbor-realm,
Perceiving the injustice, rights the wrong . . .
Infirm of purpose, they that hold the helm
Of any land, and see unmoved, for long,
A tyrant every human right o'erwhelm,
Whose name alone does blister every tongue.

My Shepherd-Host

Psalm XXII

This rolling universe below
Where healing waters rippling flow,
Is all a verdant pasture land,
Where God hath set me with His Hand.
The Lord, my Shepherd, always guides
And feeds and cares for me besides;
He ruleth me, he watcheth o'er,
And want shall I for nothing more.

And when I wander from His care,
Does He not in His Bosom bear
His wayward lamb away from blame
To Justice's path for His own Name?
For though I walk amid death's shade,
Of evil I am ne'er afraid.
Thy rod and staff they comfort me;
With me Thou art, and I in Thee.

Thou hast for me a feast prepared,
A joy with Thee and angels shared.
Anointed me with oil Thou hast,
My chalice sweet crowns my repast.
Thy mercy, Lord, shall follow me,
Until my soul from earth is free
In God's own House in bliss to dwell
Until eternity's own knell.

The Voice of Dismas

O dying Master, turn to me!
Behold my heart in sorrow bleeding;

Repentance, found in agony,
Thy gentle eyes and sight of Thee,
Have changed my curse to hopeful pleading.

Oh, let Thy mercy deign to see,
With pleading voice and heart in earnest,
A dying thief who cries to Thee,
"O Master, Lord, remember me,
When to Thy Kindom Thou returnest!"

"This day, this day, the Heavens resound
With song the hosts of Hell defying;
For by My Blood that bathes this ground
Art thou the first lost sheep I found,
The first-born fruit of My own Dying."

Makers of the Cross

When Nathan, maker of the crosses, came
Into his court with trees from Lebanon,
He found, among the cypress logs, his son,
A-smoothing one of them, a giant frame,
With patient care. Enraged, he cried: "For shame!
How many more by now you could have done!
Why shapely? Will Jehovah hang thereon?
For yours the Romans' pay will be the same
As for my other gates to Hell!"—Well may
This Jew have known that even Israel
Would nail upon the cross her God some day!
That it would be the conqueror of Hell,
And Rome, who bought it, would forever pay
A price beyond the human mind to tell.

At Calvary

Cursing, raving, crouched the whithered Old
Before the Cross. His mitre's silk and gold
Fell from the tangled, gray, disheveled hair,
Which swirled about like furies in the air.
From bulging cheeks the ashen beard did flow,
Foaming white, to leap in rage below
Upon the battered Urim, tightly pressed
Upon the heaving furnace of his breast.

And from the Hands and Feet that he had nailed,
Unheeded dripped the holy Blood that failed
To quench his flame—But still in crouching form,
His tattered purple waving in the storm,
Spat out: "Come from the Cross!"—with haughty nod—
"Come down, if Thou be He, the Son of God!"

Obedient, calmly stood the brawny new
Beneath the Cross. His plume nor broke nor blew,
But gently rested on his gleaming hood.
Staunch in his simple shining brass he stood—
His deep-set eyes stared from the lavish brow,
His face, smooth-shaven, seemed as lifeless now
As the eagle in relief upon his chest,
A noble shield that held a nobler breast.

And from the Side through which his lance he ran
The precious Fount of Life to flow began,
And washed the blindness from the deep-set eyes.
His armor shone like the golden sun that dies
At evening. Then he spoke with noble nod:
"Truly, truly, this was the Son of God!"

Easter Lilies

Well might the poet ask—Has frosted lea
Preserved some virgin snow within her breast
For Spring to blow upon her verdant crest
In clustered chalices of purity?
Or are they kisses of St. Anthony
Which on the Holy Infant's lips he pressed?
Or thoughts of babes not yet by language dressed
Or words untainted by maturity?

White—Tint of Heaven! What a Paradise
Is one wide field of lilies. Enchanting sight
The lovely mist that on the meadows lies,
As if the angels lost their pure samite,
And Easter stole the curtains of the skies
To deck His Resurrection Day in white.

Priesthood

God drew me out of nothing
    And held me in His Hand;
He draws me out of nothing
    I hold Him in my hand!

Departure

I saw a flower by your window
    After you said good-bye.
It brimmed with dew to overflowing,
    I thought it was your eye.

Its gaze could not but keep recalling
    Your eye's enchanting hue:

I cannot say what was its color,
    I know 'twas filled with dew.

Golden Stairs

To Father Lasance

Who knows but that my prayer-book,
    Which looks at me
From out its nook,
    Is aught else than it seems to be.
Perhaps it is one stepping stone
    Of many more,
With which, alone,
    A builder building o'er and o'er
Has raised a staircase to the sky!
    How bright they look,
Scaling on high,
    Each golden stair a golden book
Of golden words in golden pages—
    May you climb
Where saints and sages
    Have attained their goal sublime!

Reformation

A Monk to a Nun

Recall, O wimpled wight, the day
That joined our fingers with a rosary?
You took the beads, the cross remained to me.
But now there is no need for us to pray—
Come, leave your beads unstrung;
I have already flung
The cross away.

A King to a Maid

Sweet frailty! My word, that thou
Shouldst toil thus aught, my dear!
On afterthought, I must allow
Thy mistress be not well, I fear.
Thou couldst well flaunt her royal hems . . .
There is no Tiber nor Guadalquivir
But thou and I and Thames!

Midsummer Night's Dream

Of the Old Home Town

All was there as it was then,
The church, the priest, the booming steeple,
The altar, and the yawning people,
And the Gloria with its long Amen.

Thanatopsis

Mae intended to sleep,
But she heard all the sermon.
Though the preacher waxed deep,
Mae intended to sleep;
Then she happened to peep
    At a coat with a worm on;
Mae intended to sleep,
    But she heard all the sermon.

Communion

My Lord, my God, my All,
What joy is mine to hear it,
That You my body call
The temple of Your Spirit!

If He is lost once more,
What, Mary, is more simple,
Than to seek Him as of yore
And find Him in the temple!

Trees

"Tree-climbing is the greatest joy,"
The Good Thief said in Heaven.
"I did it since I was a boy,
Perhaps, of six or seven.

"Our rabbi grew such fruits and figs,
More fit for mouths of princes;
But I could reach the farthest twigs
And steal his choicest quinces.

"And when I grew, my worldly worries
In tree tops found their calm,
For I would enter second-stories
By stepping from a palm.

"But in his trade however good,
A thief by fate is cursed.
They led me where three tall trees stood
And hanged me on the first.

"I died a thief, as you all see,
On limbs that I had trod—
But never dreamt that from a tree
I'd steal the Heart of God."

A Shooting-Star

Lucifer! Proud falcon of the sky,
The Hunter slays you in your boastful flight;

And headlong down you tumble, followed by
A spray of feathers flashing in the night!

The Old Organ

When myriad muses on the choir loft
Respond in grandeur to the touch of art
Upon a keyboard in the chancel's heart,
The old and little organ that had oft
Poured from its reedy throat an anthem soft
Must close its lips and silently depart.
But where? To rust away or weep apart,
And nevermore its voice resound aloft?
Perhaps some humble church could dry its tears,
And join its soul to that of Poverty.
The Music Master of the whirling spheres,
Who tunes the winds upon the woods and sea,
Turns from their trembling peals and gladly hears
The honeyed droning of a little bee!

The Loving Shepherd

His lavish tresses hung before His Face,
Foremost He leans over the black abyss.
One tender hand clings to the precipice,
The other stretches down with eager grace
Toward a lamb, lost near the depthless place.
What dearer picture of His Love than this—
The Love betrayed by a defying kiss
For love imperiled o'er defying space?
Gentle Tender of the Father's Sheep!
How can I help Thee on a deed so grand?
When down the brink upon a mountain steep
Thou reachest for a wanderer of Thy band?
O let me watch by Thee beside the deep,
And, as Thou leanest downward, hold Thy Hand.

Mighty Builders

Great Cheops! Builder of the house that hid
Time's family through ages past, I know
Another who surpassed your pyramid:
My father built our little bungalow.

Portrait of a Catechist

A tender flower is a nun,
    A silken rose
Blowing in the sun
    In her prayerful repose.
You also are like unto those,
    And beautiful,
But not a rose—
    A flower indescribable.
You bloom where roses do not grow,
    In lonely lands;
And, when you blow
    Your attar on the desert sands,
The snows blush on the sierra's crest.
    God smiles above . . .
At night you rest,
    Fresh with dewdrops of His Love.

To a Young Seminarian

O Little Bo-Peep, don't weep, don't weep,
You'll know it when you grow older,
That the worldly hearts of your sheep, your sheep,
Have to wander apart if you keep, you keep,
That Lamb resting on your shoulder.

Some day you will step in the presence of kings,

And life full of gladness will be,
And your sheep will come flocking around you.
Someday you will kneel by the one King of Kings
On a Fisherman's boat by the sea,
And the Lamb that you love will attend you.

So Little Bo-Peep, don't weep, don't weep,
You'll know it when you grow older,
When again you come to your sheep, your sheep,
Everyone for your Lambkin to keep, to keep,
And you resting on His Shoulder!

The Rondeau

There were flutes once merry with stops . . .
—Witter Bynner.

A flute with stops I try to play,
Like this sweet lilting roundelay,
E'en though my fingers are so slow,
That, when into its mouth I blow,
They grope about in disarray.

I cannot stop the holes away
And blow in rhythm; and I may
Not play in tune as those who know
A flute with stops.

But still my thoughts are never gray;
Nor will I yet be led to say,
"I cannot blow or finger so,
'Tis breath and motion wasted."-No!
I'm glad I tried to play to-day
A flute with stops.

Wake Me the Birds

Despiértenme las aves
con su cantar no aprendido . . .

Wake me the birds upon the trees
 With their untutored melodies,
And I will hear rechanted there
The theme of happiness, a prayer
 I learned upon my mother's knees.

"Fear of the morrow will displease,
For God is Love, and Love foresees;
For so the birds are free from care,
  Wake me the birds.

Those golden throats upon the leas,
Those silver throats upon the seas,
 I want their anthems everywhere,
I want to be like them fore'er,
Of whom One said, "For such as these—"
  Wake me the birds.

Ring Easter Bells

Ring, Easter Bells! You lilies bright,
Pure dainty chalices of white,
Ring out the winter, bring the Spring,
And sing the newly-risen King—
Ring in the dawn, ring out the night.

Lilies of Easter! Bells bedight
With spotless sides of snow samite,
Pour forth your joyful tidings—ring,
   Ring, Easter Bells.

Make darkened hearts to burst with light,
And burdened souls to rise in flight;
Make all the world to soar and sing.
Enlightened, pure, unwearying;
Sing of the King, His Love and Might—
Ring, Easter Bells!

The Hiders

(Calderón)

God, than whose Love there is none wider,
Ready reply to all souls appealing,
Thou on this altar Thyself concealing,
Hiding to find the hider:

If me Thou seekest, need I fear it?
Come, we will find a place of hiding,
We two—my soul in thee abiding,
And Thou within my spirit.

Surprised

Out of the candle-flame it dashed upon me,
A small gray moth across my breast, a gust
Of wonder that half-walked, half-flitted on me,
Leaving behind a trail of silver dust.

Back to the candle-flame it flashed and flitted
And dropped, a pinch of ashes to the floor,
The while I stared upon my breast, outwitted
By thoughts that leave a trail, but come no more.

Lines

—On Reading a Ballad of Villon

Men, for God's love, let no gibe here be said,
But pray to God that He forgive us all.

Villon, upon the cross there was a thief!
And he spoke sorrow in his master's ear.
By one love-prayer his sins, like yours, his grief,
Were washed by penitence, like yours, a tear—

Might He not from the Book tear out your leaf
And say, "Where are the snows of yester-year?"

Reassured

The woods last night were an old, old story.
Last night the leaves were an angry sea,
And they chilled my brow as each waving bough
Rolled over and under at every tree—

"Master," I cried. "Help me, else I perish!"
But God slept on and seemed not to hear—
But then, when He woke, the one word He spoke
Rebuked me my ocean of faithless fear.

Tonight I rest reassured and happy,
The Master sleeps at my slumber's helm;
And the waves surge nigh with the peaceful sigh
Of sycamore, tamarack, oak and elm.

'Twas the Last Rose . . .

'Twas the last rose of summer
    Who came to our door,
And she brought a petition
She had not brought before.

And we lit vigil candles,
    Two hearts flaming red;
Though we knew that no blessed
Would quicken the dead.

But, faith! now the cold days
The Saint's message bring:
They have sown her to wait for
Her love in the Spring.

Sonnet from the Spanish of Calderón

All these that were once pomp and gladness gay,
Awakening the morning's rainbowed blush,
At evening will in useless sadness hush
Asleep within the night's cold arms away.

This splendor that defies the heavens' sway,
This iris striped with gold and scarlet flush,
Will be a lesson to our life's proud rush:
How much is learned within a single day!

To bloom, the roses woke and opened wide;
They bloomed and in the budding of a flower
Found tomb and cradle lying side by side;
Such did men see their fortunes and their power,
All in a day were born—and also died:
The century that passed was but an hour!

Prisoner

Life is a jail
As led by me;
And no man's bail
Can set me free.

I could cut through
My three-link chain;
Yet all that, too,
Would be in vain.

For don't you know
What I speak of?
My soul's window
Is barred with love!

Beauty and the Hidden Truth

You laugh at us, vain world, because we find
The Beauty and the hidden Truth you seek.
'Tis in the things that are to you so bleak
That Beauty lives—'tis in the soul and mind,
And not the sense.
You strip yourself of innocence
And down the Parian quarry step to view
Your naked self in Phidian chiseled chips;
You find a grim apocalypse
Of drooping roses, marble slabs, and you . . .

Climb to the mount where Beauty weeps apart,
A breathing rose-bewreathed Carraran art!
Behold how, cruciform and garmentless,
With outstretched arms He bursts to you His Heart.
Those garland hands are crumpled roses—yes,
Whose petals dripped and left a knot of thorns!
Thorns, thorns they are, and scorns!
The cause for which true Beauty mourns,
Naked, atoning for your nakedness.

Oculos Habent

"There is no Christ, there is no Christ,
Or else I would have found Him!"
A blind man cries unto the blind
Who crowd and grope around him.

"Ages ago a blind man lived
Whose sight He did restore him;
But now there is no Christ, no Christ . . ."
And Christ walks on before him.

The blind one spits upon the ground,
Trusting his vain endeavor,
And rubs the mud upon his eyes,
And sees Christ less than ever.

The Wren

God rested on the seventh day,
For He was pleased with His great deed;
And that is why, wishing to play,
He fluted out a hollow reed.

Into it wandered, so to speak,
A crumpled feather from some nest;
God smiled and blew; there came a squeak.
With quirking tail and wings and breast.

To a Diminutive Chickadee

Dwarf among your elfin kin,
And yet you top the tallest tree;
You pipe a note thinner than thin,
But loud enough to come to me.

You drop, a note, from twig to limb,
And echo back from limb to twig,
No shoot too small for each your whim,
And for your goal no tree too big.

You toil and sing for all you're worth,
Like men whose ways we profit by,
Never disgusted with the earth,
Never disheartened by the sky.

The Pagan

Saffron is a hue of glory,
And jade a color of self-love.
And this I found in an old story,
Which I had read, but not thought of.

I have an idol, unrivaled yet,
In Thibet or Hindustan;
A god of clay, but wigged with jet,
Holding an ivory fan,
Squatting, like Buddha, and slant-eyed,
Full-bellied in robes of blue,
Waiting for prayer and offering
Through rites I claim are due—
I have an amber light to hide
Full-burning at his feet,
And while I pray and bow and sing,
He beams with golden heat:
Saffron his cheeks, his nose, his chin,
And, where they cast a shade,
His breast and eyes and sallow grin
Are blue-green jade.

Saffron is a hue of glory,
And jade a color of self-love,
And this I found in an old story,
So often read . . . but not thought of . . .

Giralda

Have you seen her picture yet?
It's a secret that I let
(You smile) to very few.
Now, if you only knew
How I treasure my Giralda,
For that is what she's called—ah!
You smile again—
Verily, the fair Giralda
Is the fairest one in Spain.

In all my life I have not me
A soul who does not crave to set
His hands on what is mine.
'Tis true I have no sign
To distinguish my possession,
And so no mind's procession
Will yet refrain
From holding there a frequent session
In my tall domain.

Now you ask how I can get
Some moments there without regret?
'Tis simple to find time
(As when I pen this rhyme),
Time to enjoy this olden tower
In duty's every hour.
Moments in vain?
Perhaps—but grapes are seldom sour,
When kissed by idle rain.

Still I warn you ('tis no threat)
Please to shun my minaret.

It is wiser if you do,
It was not meant for you.
Oh, never let the fair Giralda
Make your mind run wild—ah!
You smile again—
Ah, she's fairest—La Giralda,
Of old castles in Spain.

The Angelus

Millet

Evening and prayer for Normandy.
A faded sky and steeple dim
Blend in audible harmony . . .
The man bows to his wife, and she
Bows toward him.

Evening, and I too breathe a prayer,
As silent as the peasants' own.
And ever but one sound is there—
That painted peal on painted air,
That tinted tone.

The shades of night erase the sound.
The steeple dim and fading sky
Blend into silence . . . neither ground
Nor man nor wife nor sky are found,
But God and I.

At the Holy Sepulchre

Within this hollow cave, so sad and lone
Among the silence of a garden, lies
He who is dead and who, they say, will rise
Renewed with life from out the lifeless stone.
Around it stand the hopeful trees, His own,

By which He walked; those olives, saintly-wise
With visions of Gethsemane, their eyes
A dew of tears, their lips a wind-breathed moan.

Here lies a God!—and dead because men die!
Forsaken by the very ones with whom
He let the promise of the new Life stand.
Have you no hope, O sinners, none to vie
With all these trees?—
Yet, see, close to the Tomb—
Stands Mary with a lily in her hand!

VI Station

Veronica Wipes the Face of Jesus with Her Veil

No man upon the Holy City's mart
Bears pit for the bleeding Savior's sake;
Only a woman dares those ranks to break,
Whose veil Jesus receives with silent art,
As when the sky his face deigns to impart
To the clear mantle of a crystal lake—
But sweeter far she finds it is to take,
The Image that He prints upon her heart.

Dear Lord, my heart I now return to Thee.
Make Thou my spirit as it should have been,
The peaceful surface of a peaceful sea;
Reflect Thy Holy Face so deep therein,
That blurred by ripples it may never be,
Much less effaced by any waves of sin.

Catholic Negro Spiritual

The Prophet he saw a chariot of flames
Come sailing on fiery foam;

Swung low that chariot, he stepped in the chariot,
And the chariot carried him home.

The Lawd He needs no chariot of fire,
'Cause up to the heavens' blue dome
He rose without chariot, He was His Chariot,
Sweet Chariot climbing to home.

Our Lady she sailed in the angels' hands
That lifted her out of the loam;
Light was her chariot, wings were her chariot,
Dear chariot flying to home.

Sweet Jesus, dear Mary, Elias, come down—
When I can no longer more roam—
You all be my chariot, swing low, sweet chariot,
Coming for to carry me home.

Advertisement

A beauty of fashion
    You, too, can be;
The last peak of passion,
    Quite easily.

An even complexion
    Which lines dispels;
The eyes a reflection
    Of two black wells.

White teeth and pearly,
    Thin nose and small;
A smile that so early
    Reveals them all.

You, too, can be pretty,
Be you so dull,
The depth of all beauty—
Behold a skull.

Death of a Virgin

The Beloved Who feeds among
The lilies rare
Comes with a throng
Of maidens to his garden fair.
And three of those
Close to Him pace,
Young Agnes, Rose,
And little Therese.

The three grew roses, silken-wide:
One dyed them red
The day she died,
And one wove hers around her head;
The third, to die,
Took all her flowers
And from the sky
Rained rosy showers.

They sing a song nobody knows,
Save they who trail
The Lamb, Who goes
So softly down the mystic vale;
For each was called
By Him a garden,
A garden walled—
And He the Warden.

At last they stand, waiting with Him
    Aside a bed:
Eyes that were dim
    Grow wide and fixed. (We call her dead!)
The Beloved's Hand
    Joins hers to those
    Of Agnes and
        Therese and Rose.

Baptism

The first day, when God's Spirit hovered o'er
The waters, our great universe came in.
Again It hovers as the waters pour,
And one more little world does now begin.

Eucharistic Rubáiyát

Omar, my Soul! Open thy slothful Eyes,
For even now the warming Sun does rise,
The Light of the World that melts the Night
And leaves to Lips a Taste of Paradise!

Down by the golden Tent a Light divine
Plays on the jewelled Cups of Bread and Wine,
The while a Priest bends down to beckon God,
And, lo! the One Beloved obeys his Sign!

What matter now the Night's long Sleep of Sin,
The Feasts of pleasant Praise and worldly Din,
When at the watchful Hour of Morning Thou
Dost make the Heart brim up with Love within?

O Joy that even Earth can give to me!
O Paradise enough beneath the Tree!

Where through a Loaf of Bread and Jug of Wine
Thou kissest me and I clasp Thee!

What Little Flower

What little flower are you?
I cannot tell,
For a description may but mar you.
I know full well
Your features, delicate and hazy,
A beaming beatific dimple
Petaled with that Carmel wimple,
Smiling, simple—
Like a daisy.

What little flower?
At first sight,
I know you are from Jesus' bower,
And that for many a season bright
We had no rose so rosy pink,
Nor violet so violet, lily so white,
Nor daisy with such a beatific wink.

Shepherds

When cares at night
Keep me from sleep
In my mind's sight
I count my sheep.

And as I scan
Their passing by,
I spy a Man
Who watches nigh.

A Shepherd He
Of gentle charms—
A lamb I see
Within His arms.

He looks at me,
I look at Him,
Till sheep and He
Grow misty dim.

Thus sure I am
To sleep and rest,
Just like the lamb
Upon His breast.

To a Little Orphan Girl

One day the children came to meet us,
Like little cherubs from the sky,
Framed around the holy nuns
Who came to greet us.
And of all
The little ones
You came before me and stood still,
A pretty doll
In bow and frill
And other girlish odds and ends;
And then you looked into my eye,
And we were friends.

Sometimes, when it is dark, your face comes up,
Your eyes like water in a sapphire cup,
Searching my soul the way our guardian angels do.

And then I feel a little glad
That golden hearts have closed about and gilded you.
And somewhat sad—

Because I know another little girl
Who has a combless curl,
Who never wore a bow,
And sticks her tongue at people so
From out the most paintless of homes:
Yet, her I think more fortunate,
When evening comes,
Who watches mother set each battered plate,
Or runs to meet her daddy at the gate.

The Humblest Saint

Who might be the humblest Saint?
'Tis the person who will paint
His lowly self on such a level,
As to almost canonize the devil
And usurp his royal place,
Were it not a tall disgrace
And a humiliating thing
For hell to tolerate him king.

Tabernacle Scene

Faith, Hope, and Love from Paradise
I see within a pair of eyes.

A little child kneels down before
The silent tabernacle door.

His eyes are bright with light so rare,
Because he knows Jesus is there.

Their stare is wide and fixed and sure
Of Him whose promises endure.

Their gaze is soft as if they draw
A love that melts that gaze with awe.

Faith, Hope, and Charity—these three—
Within a pair of eyes I see.

Love's Tender Prisoner

Behold Love's tender Prisoner,
None is more calm than He;
So quiet that it seems the door
Rattles the key.

Besides the door that shuts Him in
There are the chains of Love;
Such is the weight upon Himself,
He cannot move.

Who, then, will pry the prison-lock
And gain for Him release?
And who will break those heavy fetters
Piece by piece?

The priestly hand can open the door
By turning 'round the key,
But only hearts with love a-flame
Can set Him free.

Sonnet of the Via Crucis

I For me sweet Innocence is doomed to die
II Upon the cross which He receives with smiles;

III But, as He goes, He falls 'mid jeering aisles,
IV While Mary's eyes meet His, and two Hearts cry.
V He totters, Simon helps Him, passing by,
VI A woman wipes His Face, despite the files
VII Of soldiers, and again He falls 'mid riles—
VIII Yet, can console those women weeping nigh.
IX Christ, help me carry on, though oft I fall,
X And strip from me whatever earth can give;
XI Come, crucify my flesh, my will, my all,
XII And let me die for love of You, and live.
XIII In Mary may I rest after the strife,
XIV And then, entombed with You, arise to Life.

Hymn to Saint Louis

O holy King, how well thy crown
Thy noble rank to men extolls;
Yet wearest thou that robe of brown
Which Francis gives to humble souls.

Chorus:
St. Louis King, so pure, so true,
In Christ's own cause unwearying,
Teach us to fight the good fight through,
Beneath the Cross of Christ our King!

A lily shines upon thy breast,
And in thy hand a gleaming sword,
To show the world that it is best
With heart and hand to serve the Lord.

Heritage

A heritage from God is art,
The urge and power to create,

The distant thunder of the Maker's Voice
Through ages from the human heart
In varied echoes made articulate.
Let men rejoice
That God such care for men does show—
For everyone some mite of genius shares:
Da Vinci, Dante, Michaelangelo
Were nothing more than favorite heirs.

All For Love

Jesus, when the cross was brought to You,
You drew it to yourself and kissed it long,
And, oh, if You could see the passion strong
Of jealous love that in my own heart grew!

I long to stretch my arms full freely, too,
For I to You much more than trees belong;
But when I try, I fail—something is wrong,
If aught restrains me from what love would do.

My arms are loaded down, like moss-hung trees,
With bales and burdens of the things of earth.
My breast is weighted down with vanities,
With all I hold to heart of passing worth.
Here's all for love! I fling away this dross—
Sweet Jesus, come, embrace and kiss this cross!

Books by Fray Angélico Chávez

Archives of the Archdiocese of Santa Fe, 1678–1900. Washington, D.C.: The Academy of American Franciscan History, 1957.

But Time and Chance: Padre Martínez of Taos. Santa Fe: The Sunstone Press, 1981.

Chávez: A Distinctive American Clan of New Mexico. Santa Fe: William Gannon, 1989.

Clothed with the Sun. Santa Fe: Writers' Editions, 1939.

La Conquistadora, the Autobiography of an Ancient Statue. Paterson, New Jersey: St. Anthony Guild Press, 1954.

Coronado's Friars. Washington, D.C.: The Academy of American Franciscan History, 1968.

The Domínguez-Escalante Journal: Their Expedition Through Colorado, Utah, Arizona, and New Mexico in 1776. Translated by Fray Angélico Chávez and edited by Ted. J. Warner. Provo, Utah: Brigham Young University Press, 1976.

Eleven Lady-Lyrics and Other Poems. Paterson, New Jersey: St. Anthony Guild Press, 1945.

From An Altar Screen; El Retablo; Tales from New Mexico. Illustrated by Peter Hurd. New York: Farrar, Straus & Cudahy, 1957.

The Lady from Toledo. Illustrated by Fray Angélico Chávez. Fresno: Academy Guild Press, 1960.

Missions of New Mexico, 1776, A Description by Fray Francisco Atanasio Domínguez with Other Contemporary Documents. Translated and annotated by Eleanor B. Adams and Fray Angélico Chávez. Albuquerque: University of New Mexico Press, 1956.

My Penitente Land: Reflections on Spanish New Mexico. Albuquerque: University of New Mexico, Press. 1974.

New Mexico Triptych. Being Three Panels and Three Accounts: 1. The Angel's New Wings; 2. The Penitente Thief; and 3. Hunchback Madonna. Illustrated by Fray Angélico Chávez. Paterson, New Jersey: St. Anthony Guild Press, 1940.

Origins of New Mexico Families in the Spanish Colonial Period. In Two Parts: The Seventeenth (1598–1693) and the Eighteenth (1693–1921) Centuries. With four illustrations by José Cisneros. Santa Fe: The Historical Society of New Mexico, 1954.

The Oroz Codex; or Relations of the Description of the Holy Gospel Province in New Spain and the Lives of the Founders and Other Note-worthy Men of Said Province Composed by Fray Pedro Oroz: 1584–1586. Washington, D.C.: The Academy of American Franciscan History, 1972.

Our Lady of the Conquest. Albuquerque: University of New Mexico Press, 1948.

Selected Poems with An Apologia. Santa Fe: Press of the Territorian, 1969.

Seraphic Days; Franciscan Thoughts and Affections on the Principal Feasts of Our Lord and Our Lady and All the Saints of the Three Orders of the Seraph of Assisi. Detroit: Duns Scotus College, 1940.

The Single Rose; the Rose Unica and Commentary of Fray Manuel de Santa Clara. Santa Fe: Los Santos Bookshop, 1948.

The Song of Francis. Illustrated by Judy Graese. Flagstaff: Northland Press, 1973.

Très Macho—He Said. Padre Gallegos of Albuquerque, New Mexico's First Congressman. Santa Fe: William Gannon, 1985.

The Virgin of Port Lligat. Fresno, California: Academy Literary Guild, 1959.

When the Santos Talked: A Retablo of New Mexico Tales. Drawings by Peter Hurd. Santa Fe: William Gannon, 1977.